Brain Blunders:

Discover Your Flawed Logic, Failures in Common Sense and Intuition, and Irrational Behavior - *How to Think Less Stupid*

By Peter Hollins,
Author and Researcher at
petehollins.com

Table of Contents

Chapter 1. Misadventures of the Human Brain

When I was a teenager, I remember going with my parents to buy a new car.

The car certainly wasn't for me, no matter how much I begged and pleaded with the might of my newly minted driver's license. The car was for my mother; she had gotten into a minor accident, which our insurance company had deemed *major* enough to cover the cost of a new car. Many years later, it is still one of the few positive interactions I would ever have with insurance companies.

I distinctly remember this day because I remember the salesperson that we dealt with—or rather *tolerated*. If you could create an untrustworthy salesperson in a lab, you would come up with this man. If you looked up the word "sleazy" in the dictionary, his picture would be next to it. He was the stereotype of a slimy salesman who would pat your back and keep repeating your name in an annoying fashion. His palms were sweaty and he shook your hand for far too long. It was like he had read all the advice of what *not* to do in sales and taken it as a challenge.

Things moved quickly because my parents were in a buying mood and it showed plainly on their faces. They were busy people and just wanted to get in, get the car, and get out. This type of sentiment is like blood in the water for salespeople, who want motivated customers that actually spend money.

We took a quick test drive and into the office we went to talk about exactly what model was desired and what the end price would be. I noted that the salesman didn't bring up the price until as late in the process as possible. Every time my father tried to clarify, he would say something like, "Of course, we'll get to that right after this. I promise. Just a couple more things to hammer out."

He was doing this to draw my parents deeper into the process so as to gain their emotional investment in the car. When he finally presented the price with all the amenities my parents wanted (power windows, air-conditioning, a CD player, heated seats), he presented a figure that made my parents gasp. In particular, my father looked shell-shocked, like he had just witnessed a puppy being kicked.

The salesman had done his best to anchor the price exceedingly high, so even if my parents wanted to negotiate, they would have to start there and end up far higher than they wanted to. In other words, because the quoted price was high, it was innately assumed that you couldn't work too far down from it.

This might have worked on other people, but not my parents, who still kept things that were years past their expiration date "just in case." Stingy would be an understatement. Not only that, but my parents were raised in a culture where you were mocked if you paid the sticker price on anything and didn't try to get a good deal. They had grown up going to local markets, and haggling was second nature to them.

My parents set their own price, which was as aggressively low as the salesman's was aggressively high, and it was the salesman's turn to gasp. He began to squawk about all the costs involved, but my father didn't take the bait; he simply reached into a folder he had brought with him and showed printouts of prices from other dealerships that were more in line with his own. He stood up, saying, "I guess they will get my business. It's too bad. We liked you."

In what appeared to be the salesman's final argument to seal the deal at a higher price, he tried to get me on his side by appealing to my sense of desperation of wanting to drive. He said things like, "Kid, if your father doesn't pull the trigger here, he'll never get the prices at the other places and you won't be able to hang out with your friends!" Little did he know I had a strict curfew and could never hang out with my friends regardless. He had tried to make an ally out of me, but I already disliked him, so I would never have agreed with him.

At this point, my parents started walking out and discussing the address for the next dealership, as well as how much they wanted a car that very day. The salesman started pursuing, and in the end, my parents walked out with the car they wanted at the price they wanted. (That car ended up being passed down to me some years later, and I found it profoundly funny that my parents had left the price sticker on the interior top of the front windshield as a reminder of their triumph that day.)

This battle of wills was forever emblazoned in my brain as an example of how people can be seduced into behaviors and thoughts that are completely contrary to what they want. The salesman was trying to raise the price while my parents were trying to lower the price; each side wanted to use a sneaky fallacy in thinking to achieve a specific outcome by clouding judgment. They were each trying to bend reality without tipping the other off.

But really, humans don't need help with clouding our judgment, thinking, reasoning, and perception. We make poor decisions and exhibit seriously flawed thinking on a daily basis. Our brains try so hard to make sense of the world that it actually works against them. Combine that with emotional thinking and a tendency to jump to conclusions and what do you get?

Well, us: overdeveloped primates with profoundly flawed brains that make suboptimal decisions. Humans really don't see the world as it is, and this isn't just due to a difference in opinions or experiences. We have to realize that our brains have a very different purpose than clear and accurate thinking; it wants pure pleasure, survival, and energy maintenance—not terms that often overlap with good judgment.

That would be like depending on your taste buds to make healthy decisions about diet. That's not their purpose! Your taste buds just want to enjoy themselves and taste what they were designed to taste, regardless of the fat content or number of calories. We can't very well judge nutrition through how good something tastes because of fat, oil, and grease.

It's hard to overlook millennia of programming to see the world only in terms of, well, figurative fat, oil, and grease. This can result in funny one-time occurrences or massive errors with damaging consequences. We think we are driven by logic and reason, but it appears that common sense isn't really as common as we'd like to think.

This book is a manual to the general misjudgment of your brain and why we do what we do in such peculiar and incorrect ways. Wouldn't it be nice to see the world as it really is and, most importantly, use that accurate information to make your decisions with?

The brain shows its bias as a selfish little monster in small, almost imperceptible ways.

For instance, if you've ever been in the middle of a sentence and your mind suddenly went blank, or if you've walked into a room and suddenly forgotten what you were doing there, you've experienced what is generally known as a *brain fart*. It's not because your memory is going or a sign of early-onset Alzheimer's; it's an intentional (from your brain's perspective) lapse in cognition, judgment, and overall thought. It's as if your mind was an Etch A Sketch and the brain made the call to shake and clear it.

It might feel like an instance where you have just slipped into stupidity, but there is actually a well-founded physiological explanation for your lapses.

Neuroscientists have discovered that roughly 30 seconds before your *brain fart*, there is a decrease in blood flow to the portion of your brain that is involved in focus and attention. In other words, our brains go on autopilot because we are engaging in something that doesn't require our full focus or attention—for example, an activity such as driving, sorting your laundry, or walking the dog or any other type of behavior where your brain can be driven by instinct, muscle memory, or pure habit. These are instances where we *zone out* because your brain isn't proactively being used. Everything is familiar, and your brain is well-conditioned to react to most contingencies in these situations. Therefore, attention is not deemed necessary.

Remember how I said our brains only want to feel pleasure with little regard for the rest of our bodies? The brain is just trying to get by with as little energy expenditure as possible. When the brain senses it can let its guard down and relax because a repetitive or monotonous task is at hand, it takes a break and conserves energy, and blood flow is decreased as a reaction. The tendency for brain farts stems from a focus on energy conservation for the brain that can lead to lost laundry and even traffic accidents because of our autopilot mode.

This is akin to turning the gas and electricity off in your home at night while people are sleeping in the hopes that no one will need them. You want to keep your utilities bill as low as possible. However, what happens when someone needs to use the phone to call 911 because they are having a heart attack? You may have lowered your utilities bill a little bit, but at what cost? Well, at the very least, disrupted thinking.

The brain, while only roughly 2% of the body's weight, consumes roughly 20% of its energy and glucose expenditure. It makes sense that the brain would be so lazy whenever it is possible. Keep this in mind as we go through the following chapters and explore flawed thinking and brain blunders. It's certainly not due to stupidity or lesser intelligence; we are all just victims of how our brains function (and fail us) and need to consciously fight back.

Chapter 2. What Free Will?

No people prefer to think of themselves as followers. We all like to imagine that we have *free will* and are actively making our decisions instead of the other way around.

In fact, we view followers with a negative slant. These are the people who are easily influenced by others and can even be manipulated into doing things they're either unaware of or uninterested in. Whatever the case, followers are not people that are seen in an attractive light.

On the other hand, there are *leaders*. Leaders are what we typically want to aspire to—and for good reason. They have power and independence. Leaders blaze the trail and set the path instead of the other way around. They are strong-minded and are driven by a set of morals and convictions. Above all else, they do what they want out of their own free will, not because someone has told them to do it. If you want to compliment someone in a work setting, you would call them a leader, and if you want to insult someone, you would call them a follower.

We all want to be leaders on some level because we want to feel that we are in charge of our destinies, but the truth of how we all act is a bit uglier. We really just can't help but subconsciously follow the people around us, whether we want to or not. It influences a substantial part of what we want and the way we think, despite our best attempts to be an individual thinker. Of course, the brain contributes with its tendency to be lazy.

Here's a simple and relatable example.

If you walk into your new job and you find everyone wearing magenta shirts, you are probably going to buy a magenta shirt as soon as you can, despite the fact that there is no dress code and no one has ever mentioned anything about magenta shirts. Something in your mind will tell you that you should be conforming to the people around you, even though there are no rules about it and the people you've asked haven't mentioned it, either. You could argue that your free will directs you to dress like the others, but in reality, wasn't it heavily influenced by the general consensus? Aren't they indistinguishable at some point?

In a 2019 study published in the scientific journal *Nature*, Australian researchers found that through monitoring brain activity with an fMRI machine, they were able to predict choices that test subjects made a full 11 seconds before they consciously declared their choices. This seems to imply that thoughts and intentions exist unconsciously before they ever become conscious. If the brain prepares to act before you are consciously aware you're making a choice, then what is free will, really?

This might verge into the philosophical a bit too much for this book, but let's leave it at this: we are so heavily influenced by the people around us and the contexts we find ourselves in that free will is more accurately described as a choice we *think* we are independently making. We are unable to separate ourselves from what surrounds us, sometimes to our detriment. Sometimes it works to our benefit, but other times, it squashes independent, innovative, and insightful thinking.

In this chapter, I want to cover some infamous landmark psychological studies that show just how little our actions are determined by free will and instead are decided by context, social pressure, or outright instruction. These studies shed light on why we feel compelled to wear a magenta shirt even if there is no dress code and why people tend to act against their own interests or values. They speak to our brains' compulsions of survival via not standing out and conserving energy.

The Asch Conformity Experiment

The first study that digs deep into the concept of dubious free will is the Asch Conformity Experiment. It was conducted by Solomon Asch of Swarthmore College in the 1950s and broadly demonstrated the compulsion to conform and "fit in" despite our best instincts and interests.

The study was relatively simple and asked participants to engage in a vision test. In each run of the study, there was only one subject, and the rest of the people present were Asch's confederates. They would attempt to influence the true participant to conform and act against their free will. The participant sat around a table with seven confederates and was asked two questions:

1. Which line was the longest in Exhibit 2?
2. Which line from Exhibit 2 matches the line from Exhibit 1?

Below is what the participants saw and made their judgment on. When participants were asked this question alone, through writing or without confederates who would provide a range of answers, they consistently answered in the exact same way: obviously Line C and Line A, respectively.

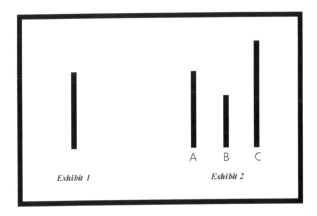

However, when confederates were present and provided incorrect answers, what followed was surprising.

When the true participant was surrounded by confederates who gave incorrect answers, such as stating that Line C was equal to Exhibit 1 or Line B was the longest in Exhibit 2, they also conformed their answers to be stunningly incorrect based on the social pressures of the people around them. Over one-third of the true participants gave an obviously wrong answer, presumably because of the influence of peer pressure and the general feeling of "What could I be missing that everyone else is seeing?" This feeling of confusion and wanting to avoid appearing stupid can cause someone to conform to something obviously wrong, which will actually make them appear stupid because they were trying to avoid that very thing. Asch successfully displayed that people, whether they believe it or not, wish to blend in with their peers and their environment so they don't stick out.

People don't want to commit a faux pas, so even if they thought the line was truly the same length or not, they made it seem like they did. Follow-ups to Asch's experiment showed that this effect increased when more confederates were present. If there were one or two confederates who gave incorrect answers, the effects were small, but if there were more than two, then people seemed to feel a significantly greater sense of peer pressure. It seems there is comfort in numbers—if three people see something a certain way, then I might be the one missing something, but if only one person disagrees with me, then they are equally as likely as me to be missing something.

Asch commented, "The tendency to conformity in our society is so strong that reasonably intelligent and well-meaning young people are willing to call white black." He had the opportunity to ask participants after the experiment whether they actually believed their altered stances, and most did not and simply wanted to go along with the group because they did not want to be thought of as "peculiar." Others thought the group's judgment was actually correct and felt their new answer to be correct as well.

These two approaches represent the two main reasons people appeared to conform and act against their own free will. First, they wanted to be liked by the group and not seen as a "peculiar" outsider—this is called a *normative influence*. They wanted to fit in and be seen as comparable to the group. Second, they conformed because they thought their information was faulty, and they wanted to use the group's judgment instead of their own. This is called an *informational influence*, where they doubted their own instincts and assumed others had more and better information than they did.

In either case, people's sense of free will is subverted by emotional reactions to what other people are doing. You can say that you chose to go along with other people's answers consciously, but in fact, it wasn't what you truly wanted to do. Does free will exist if it is squashed as a mere thought?

This is how we end up wearing magenta shirts far more often than we think we should. You might start with buying only one, but by the end of a year, you'll probably have a closet full of magenta shirts just because it seems like the right thing to do to fit in. You want acceptance from the group to not appear "peculiar," and you feel there's a reason magenta is so prevalent, one you don't quite know yet.

It might not be a surprise that we take cues on how to behave and think from other people, especially if it's a situation that is foreign to us. For instance, if you show up at a fancy ball, you would look to how other people bow, stand, and interact so you can calibrate your own behavior. Where this takes a deviation into subverting free will is where you go directly against what you know to be true just to conform. Asch's experiment was one instance where a clearly correct answer was passed over, showing the true power of peer pressure and social influence.

The psychological implications of Asch's experiment may not be groundbreaking— we are all afraid of judgment, but the degree to which we strive to avoid it is huge and can be said to make us a follower in a negative way.

Milgram's Shock Experiment

Stanley Milgram's experiment chronicled in his 1963 paper "Obedience to Authority: An Experimental View" is one of the most important and famous psychological experiments ever conducted. And for our purposes, it demonstrates how we are slaves to authority and generally don't act in a way we want when ordered to do something under the guise of a duty. In more recent times, remembering the conclusions of Milgram's experiment can explain how atrocities as unthinkable as torture of prisoners of war have happened or even how genocide was allowed to occur during World War II.

The people committing such atrocities are always villainized, and yet they may not have been inherently *evil*. Instead, Milgram showed us another explanation as to why people can act in appalling manners while still remaining very human at heart. It can serve as a general lesson on why people who are capable or who have done dark things aren't different from you or me.

Milgram began his research at Yale University in the 1960s with the initial impetus of studying the psychology of genocide. He began to theorize that people weren't necessarily evil, twisted, or even different from those who *didn't* commit genocide but that it was rather a reflection of authority, orders, and the perception of a lack of accountability. In other words, if you were just being told what to do and you were conditioned to follow orders without question, there was a pretty good chance you were going to be able to do anything.

After all, that is the reason soldiers go through boot camp and are berated endlessly by drill instructors—it is a process designed to promote obedience and conformity, even in the worst conditions that combat will present.

However, Milgram's experiment showed it wasn't only trained soldiers who could fall victim to such blind obedience and have their free will taken away from them. Milgram built a "shock machine" that looked like a device that would be used to dole out torture, but in reality, it did nothing and was mostly a series of lights and dials. This would be his tool for exposing human nature.

His experiment worked on the premise that the participant was administering a memory test to someone in another room, and if the unseen person made a mistake on the test, the participant was given the instruction from a man in a lab coat to punish them with electric shocks stemming from the "shock machine." The shocks would escalate in intensity based on how many wrong answers were given. Before the start of the experiment, the participant was given a 45-volt electric shock that was attached to the shock machine. Forty-five volts was where the shocks would begin and then increase in 15-volt increments with each mistake. The shock machine maxed out at 450 volts, which also had a warning label reading "Danger: Severe Shock" next to it, and the final two switches were also labeled "XXX."

The unseen test-taker was actually an actor who followed a script of getting the vast majority of the questions incorrect. As the participant administered shocks, goaded on and encouraged by the man in the white lab coat, the actor would cry out loudly and begin to express pain and anguish, begging them to stop and then eventually falling completely silent.

Despite this, pushed on by the man in the white lab coat, a full 62% of participants administered the electrical shocks up to the highest level, which included the "XXX" and "Danger" levels. Milgram only allowed the man in the white lab coat to encourage with neutral and relatively benign statements such as "Please continue" and "It is absolutely essential that you continue."

The participants weren't coerced to, in their perception, shock someone to unconsciousness or death! Sixty-two percent reached the 450-volt limit, and none of the subjects stopped before reaching 300 volts. At 315 volts, the unseen actors went silent. The participants weren't being forced to do this, neither were they being yelled at or threatened. How could these results have occurred?

Are people just callous and have little regard for human life and suffering outside of their own? That can't be true. What's more likely to be true is how persuasive the perception of authority can be in subverting our free will. We will act against our wishes if we sense that we are being ordered to by someone who has power over us, no matter how arbitrary.

This obedience to authority and sense of deference can even push us to electrocute an innocent person to implied death. Suddenly, things such as genocide, the Holocaust, and torturing prisoners of war didn't seem so far-fetched. We like to think we have hard limits on what we could inflict on others, but the results of Milgram's experiments showed otherwise—our free will was completely bypassed because of a simple display of authority.

Milgram noted other factors might include the feeling that because there was an authority figure, they would hold no accountability and be able to say, "Well, he told me to!" When the participants were reminded they held responsibility for their actions, almost none of them wanted to continue participating in the experiment, and many even refused to continue if the man in the white lab coat didn't take explicit responsibility. Additionally, it was an unseen victim they had never met before, so there was a degree of separation and dehumanization that allowed actions to go further.

In the end, a normal person was shown to have followed orders given by another ordinary person in a white lab coat with a semblance of authority, which culminated in killing another person. It was quite the discovery in terms of what drives and motivates people. It was a very powerful piece of evidence that our free will is subject to all manners of delusion and influence.

The Stanford Prison Experiment

The infamous Stanford Prison Experiment was conducted on the campus of Stanford University by prominent psychologist Philip Zimbardo in 1973, and he wanted to examine a few hypotheses.

Similar to the Milgram Shock Experiments, Zimbardo wanted to test how the presence of roles of authority would drive people to do things drastically out of their nature and into an area some might call sadistic and horrible. He specifically wanted to investigate whether the brutality that was being reported in prisons throughout the nation was because the prisons had a tendency to attract sadistic people or because of the artificial environment they were placed in containing an inherent power differential. Whatever the case, it was clear that something was happening in those environments to the detriment of the prisoners.

Zimbardo found participants and randomly assigned them the role of prisoner or prison guard in a simulated jail complex built on the university campus. He theorized that if they all acted in nonaggressive ways, then abuse was happening in prison institutions because of the inherent bad actors and biased population—not because of the toxic environment. If the participants acted the same as guards and prisoners did in real prisons, that would be an argument for the corrupting influence of the prison environment itself.

Both groups of participants were told to adhere to their roles as closely as possible, though it quickly became clear the guards did this far more zealously than the prisoners. The guards wore sunglasses to avoid making eye contact, they punished prisoners who misbehaved by assigning them to solitary confinement cells, and they only referred to prisoners by their identification numbers instead of their names. In addition, the prisoners were stripped naked, showered in front of each other, and only given prison clothes. This was as close to prison environment as was possible.

This next part was critical: the guards were given free rein to do whatever they felt was necessary to maintain a functional prison cell, maintain order, and maintain respect from the prisoners. There was no physical violence allowed, but there were certainly many other ways bad behavior began to leak out. For instance, the guards would awaken the prisoners at 2:30 in the morning just because they wanted to show control and dominance. Forced push-ups until collapse were not uncommon as a form of punishment and general breaking of the spirit.

The guards embraced their roles, which caused the prisoners to embrace theirs. They began to act exactly like prisoners act in real prisons by ganging up against other prisoners, trying to curry favor with the guards, and taking the rules very seriously. One prisoner went on a hunger strike to try to gain better treatment for the prisoners, but his cohorts didn't rally behind him; rather, they viewed him as a troublemaker who was going to cause them problems if he didn't stop. They dehumanized the prisoners to an extent that cruelty became completely justifiable and acceptable.

Very quickly, the treatment of the prisoners by the guards became worse and spiraled into near-abuse. Toilet facilities became a privilege instead of a basic human right, with access to the bathroom being frequently denied, and the inmates often had to clean the facilities with their bare hands. Prisoners were stripped naked and subjected to sexual humiliation.

These were normal people put into roles with a huge power differential. Despite how good many of the guards felt they were, the majority didn't object to this treatment of the prisoners, and Zimbardo estimated one-third of the guards began to spiral into extremely sadistic behavior and thought patterns. Free will be damned—people began to play the roles they were assigned. People may not be inherently evil or sadistic, but when put into powerful positions over people that are sufficiently dehumanized, they tend to act in predictable ways.

The Stanford Prison Experiment was slated to run for 14 days, but Zimbardo felt it had to end by the sixth day. The behavior was growing out of control. People began to identify with their roles in horrifying and negative ways. The guards took the modicum of power they had and expanded it as much as possible while the prisoners became more dejected over time. Although prison guards in a vacuum may be as sensitive and courteous as the rest of us, the roles they inhabit take a toll on how they view others.

The guards egged each other on, and their behavior kept degrading because of a mob mentality. Zimbardo had neatly answered his question of whether it was situational or personal factors that contributed to the abuse rampant in the country's prison systems. When people are put into specific roles, they will live up to that role, plain and simple. It doesn't necessarily matter what someone's normal temperament is. People's free will is again undermined or pushed to the side in order to fulfill the duties of a role, to blend in, and to meet others' expectations.

These three experiments—Asch, Milgram, and Zimbardo—prove the simple fact that who we think we are doesn't matter. What matters more in determining how we will act are our surroundings, contacts, and a unique set of pressures that come with each context. Our typical definition of free will is one that allows us to dictate the path we force through life. Unfortunately, these three experiments show you what we want to do and what our will is don't match up so frequently.

We are making conscious choices, but they aren't the ideal choices we want to make—and that's a lack of free will.

Clever Hans and the Ideomotor Effect

The final way that a lack of free will comes from our peculiar brains is the *ideomotor effect.* This phenomenon occurs when our unconscious minds transform our expectations into reality through involuntary physical reactions; we do it to ourselves, other people do it to us, and this all results in a confusing carousel wheel where it's impossible to determine what is the true cause or reason for an act. One thing is for sure—it's not our conscious choice.

The emphasis here is on the words "unconscious" and "involuntary." Because we don't know we're causing the actions and we cannot control them, the results can be surprising—for others and for ourselves—and can even trick us into thinking there's magic or supernatural forces at work. As one might expect, there is another, more logical explanation.

Perhaps the most famous example of the ideomotor effect at work is the story of Clever Hans. Clever Hans was a horse that many believed could perform intellectual tasks such as telling time and doing basic math, for example. During the early 1900s, the horse's owner Wilhelm von Osten made Hans somewhat of a celebrity by carting him around Germany and showcasing his "talents" to the public. The performance would go something like this: Osten would ask the horse to calculate the sum of five plus three, and Clever Hans would tap his hoof eight times. Of course, the crowd would go wild, and von Osten would praise the horse for his superior intellect.

Not everyone believed Clever Hans was so smart, though. The German Board of Education along with psychologists Carl Stumpf and Oskar Pfungst decided to get to the bottom of the horse's unusual behavior. They designed an experiment to determine if the horse could perform the same tasks under different circumstances. After testing Hans under many different conditions, they discovered that he answered correctly only when he could see his prompter and only when the prompter knew the answer to the question being asked.

In other words, Hans couldn't add two plus two, but when asked by someone who could, he would tap four times, provided he could see the questioner. The researchers further surmised that the questioners would change their body language and posture as the horse was tapping out the answer. This altered stance occurred in unconscious anticipation of Hans arriving at the correct answer. The questioner would change their stance again upon the arrival of the final tap, providing a visual cue for Hans to stop. The questioners hoped Hans would answer correctly, which caused them to behave as if he would, and so he did.

Who is exercising free will in this situation? None of the human parties, anyway. The intention may match the result, but it's a choice that is not independently made.

The ideomotor effect is similar to a self-fulfilling prophecy. You've probably heard Henry Ford's famous quote, "If you think you can or if you think you can't, you're right." It's become a popular motivational saying used to encourage people to think positively so that their positive thoughts bring about positive behaviors. It may sound overly simplistic, but it actually works. (Try it!)

When you genuinely believe you can do something, you're actually more likely to achieve the goal. The reverse is true, too. When you doubt your abilities, your abilities are automatically compromised. Keep telling yourself you'll never get a promotion at work, for instance, and you likely never will. Self-fulfilling prophecies occur (and frequently!) because thoughts are powerful things that can indeed affect reality.

A self-fulfilling prophecy is a lot like thinking yourself into a result, good or bad. You make a prediction—or "prophecy"—about what you think is likely to happen and begin acting as if your prediction has already occurred, which in turn causes it to actually happen. For instance, consider bachelor Ted who agrees to go out on a date with Claire, a woman he believes to be way out of his league. He tells himself the date will be a disaster because Claire will immediately recognize that he's not good enough for her. He worries about this prediction all the way to the bar, and by the time he gets there, he's sweating bullets. He opens his mouth to greet her, and no words come out. He completely freezes, which weirds Claire out, setting the disastrous tone for the rest of the evening.

Would it have gone differently had Ted never predicted a catastrophic first date in the first place? Absolutely!

The ideomotor effect is also similar to *confirmation bias*, a cognitive tendency to recall or search for information that confirms something you already believe to be true. For example, if you believe everyone at your job hates you, you'll look for instances in which coworkers respond sharply to you or supervisors criticize your work. Mentally, you'll prove your theory— at least to yourself—that no one likes you. Everyone is susceptible to confirmation bias—even scientists—and the more powerful the belief, the more likely it is that confirmation bias will take hold.

Where the ideomotor effect differs from cognitive phenomena like self-fulfilling prophecies and confirmation bias is in its ability to cause an immediate physical reaction in addition to a cognitive one. The idea that an unconscious thought can trigger an involuntary reaction may seem disturbing, but it happens all the time.

The ideomotor effect is responsible for many people's staunch belief in Ouija boards, for example. People who have used these boards may swear the planchette is moving on its own when really the participant is unconsciously moving it via the ideomotor effect in order to fulfill their subconscious expectations. It's important to note that these expectations (and of course the resulting muscular movements) are not voluntary, and the participants don't know they're causing the movement.

Thus, when asked, they'll report that the planchette was moving itself (or was moved by a spirit or ghost). So while Ouija boards aren't proof that we can communicate with the dead, they are proof that our unconscious thoughts and expectations are much more powerful than we may have ever realized!

Dowsing rods work in a similar way. For centuries, pseudoscientists have claimed to be able to use rods of varying types to locate various things like oil, precious metals, and groundwater, for instance. Though they claim to have some sort of divine power, what they're really experiencing is another unintended consequence of the ideomotor effect.

Put simply, their bodies are reacting involuntarily to the expectations in their minds regarding where something might be, causing a muscle twitch that then causes the rod to point in a particular direction. Real science has repeatedly proven the results of dowsing to be unreliable.

The ideomotor effect isn't just the stuff of horror movies and variety shows, though. It has had many other real-world manifestations, and not all of them have been innocent. On the contrary, some have had heart-breaking and even life-ending consequences. For instance, in the case of facilitated communication, loved ones of those suffering from severe mental or physical conditions such as retardation or cerebral palsy that prohibit them from speaking have been fooled into thinking these patients can communicate with them by signaling a facilitator who then types on a keyboard.

Despite continual warnings from the American Psychological Association (APA) that facilitated communication has no scientific basis, many people still hold on to false hope that their debilitated friends and family members are really communicating with them through some medium. In many cases, people are grateful to the facilitators at first for helping them communicate with the person they love. Imagine their despair, though, when they eventually find out that it was nothing but a farce.

Then there's the case of Brit Jim McCormick, who was convicted of fraud in 2013 for selling fake bomb detectors to countries around the world, including Iraq, Syria, and Mexico. He claimed the devices could detect bombs, even if they were very far away or buried underground. As it turns out, the gadgets did nothing at all, except act as a catalyst for the ideomotor effect. It is said that hundreds of lives were lost because of the ruse.

Remember, though, in many cases—maybe even most cases—those who succeed in deceiving others with the ideomotor effect do so unwittingly and never realize the truth behind their antics.

For instance, facilitators who claim to help invalids communicate think they're helping both the patient and his or her loved ones. They're genuinely not trying to trick anyone; they're simply naïve. Often, they continue to believe their own "lie" even after being proven wrong by reputable scientists over and over again. Even Wilhelm von Osten had nothing to gain by making Hans a show pony; he never charged a dime for the horse's performances. These aren't bad people trying to pull the wool over the world's eyes. They're just human beings who happen to have fallen victim to the ideomotor effect.

Some people may find it disconcerting to discover just how convincing the brain can be at deception.

After all, look how foolish von Osten seems in retrospect to believe a horse could do math! And what about the spectators? How could all of those people collectively believe in something that could clearly never happen? Scary, right? There is a silver lining, though. When one is aware of how the brain operates, he or she becomes less susceptible to its trickery. In fact, the only way to outsmart the brain is to simply not trust it. Weighing subjective perceptions against cold, hard facts and concrete data is the only way to avoid being duped by our own minds and see things with any semblance of clarity.

There you have it—the ideomotor effect in action. Free will is our conscious and unfiltered intention set into action. Here, we can see that our unconscious can easily take control in ways we have zero awareness of. Whatever choice you think you are making independently is only a compendium of social and unconscious factors.

Takeaways:

- One of the first ways our brain plays tricks on us is the illusion of free will. We want it, and most of the time, we think we have it. But we don't, because our opinions are inevitably shaped by the people around us. They can cause us to do things we wouldn't do on our own, and yet we appear to be actively choosing to engage in them. Granted, this is mostly unconscious, but can you really be said to have free will if your actions and decisions aren't completely independent? Perhaps that is a question for philosophers rather than people exploring our brain's quirks.
- The Asch Conformity Experiment showed that we are under immense amounts of pressure to fit in and avoid judgment. Peer and social pressure is a powerful shaper of not only our decisions but what we perceive to be

normal reality. It's just impossible to think in a vacuum, unfortunately.

- Stanley Milgram's Shock Experiment further showed that independent thinking is the exception rather than the rule. Specifically, it showed that the perception of authority can completely rob us of our free will, even if that authority isn't real or legitimate. We simply listen and react. All we need is a veneer of plausible deniability and innocence, and we can be pushed to extreme actions.

- The Stanford Prison Experiment demonstrated the power that instructions and roles can play in our free will. We turn out to be a product of our environments. This study, along with the others, would seem to imply that nurture wins over nature most of the time.

- Finally, we are affected by the ideomotor effect. This is a psychological phenomenon in which our unconscious desires manifest through physical action—for instance, Clever Hans the horse and the humans that would signal to him. Is our unconscious desire free will? Does free will only regard our actions? Whatever the case, it's clear that, more often than not, action does not match up to intention here.

Chapter 3. Chasing Ghosts

If you were to ask 100 people if they believe in ghosts, how many do you think would say yes? It might depend on the age range or geographic location, but overall it likely wouldn't be a majority.

When faced with such a direct proposition, you might find only a low percentage is willing to admit it. But just because people will laugh at ghosts and monsters under the bed doesn't mean that they don't possess different (but ultimately extremely similar) types of magical thinking and supernatural beliefs—all of which can generally be explained or labeled as *magic*.

For instance, do you want your favorite sports team to win? You might just feel better if you wear the same pair of socks you wore the last time they won. Magical thinking such as superstitions creeps into our lives in small, almost imperceptible ways that make it second nature for us to believe in. From there, they only grow in ways that can end up skewing reality.

Essentially, *the supernatural* has become a catch-all umbrella term for things that lack a conventional explanation. There may not always be a clear explanation, but attributing what is not immediately explainable turns out to be a tendency of the human brain to jump to conclusions and make sense out of a situation—even if the explanation must be fabricated. We fabricate explanations because of an overwhelming desire to feel *in control*; if we can explain something, then we can ostensibly affect its outcome.

This is quite a comforting feeling, as opposed to feeling that you are helpless to the forces around you. When we feel we have control, we gain a sense of empowerment and agency around our lives. If we believe what we do makes a difference, then we will *do* more. For example, the superstitions surrounding sports teams. You may logically know that you aren't making a real difference, but it still feels *better* and *more comfortable* if you engage in those acts. By avoiding discomfort little by little, this tendency grows stronger.

You've likely read about this tendency when learning about ancient and not-so-ancient civilizations. The Greeks assigned a deity to nearly everything as a scapegoat or savior, and Native Americans engaged in rain dances to help their crops flourish for the coming harvest. All modern religion tends to explain the conventionally unexplainable.

We depend on supernatural beliefs because they give us a semblance of control and allow us to answer universal questions such as "How does this work?" and "Why did this happen?" Humans don't like to feel that we are random molecules of carbon and hydrogen that happened to coalesce and form somehow—we might be, but it sure feels better if we have a purpose.

Why Do We Wear Stinky Socks to Support Our Favorite Sports Team?

Superstitions are the first way we are *chasing ghosts*—that is, to create an explanation for the unexplained.

Specifically, superstitions are behaviors or thought patterns that people engage in because they believe there is a cause-and-effect relationship. You engage in superstitious acts because you believe it will get you closer to a specific outcome. For instance, if you notice that your favorite football team has won the past three times you've worn red underwear, a new superstition will be born: red underwear only on game days. You might not affect the game itself, but it appears that there is a pattern of causation, so you're going to adhere to it—sometimes even subconsciously. (Of course, the vast majority of superstitions end up being a self-fulfilling prophecy at best, where you do indeed create the outcome you were seeking, but only because you held that belief, not because of the action itself.)

Classical conditioning is the cause of many superstitions we hold throughout our lives. We commit an act, we see an outcome, and we begin to link the two, even though it's no more than a correlation or simple coincidence. It only needs to happen once or twice for you to begin to subconsciously latch onto this so-called relationship. Yet surprisingly to some sports fans, sitting in the same chair while watching matches likely does not affect the end outcome just because it happened twice three years ago. This is also why people don't walk under ladders—because negative occurrences have coincided with that event—never mind the fact that walking under a ladder puts you directly into the path of falling debris and traps you from moving to safety.

Yet these beliefs are what humans cling to because it brings clarity to an otherwise random and chaotic world. This tendency even extends to pigeons, as the famous psychologist B.F. Skinner proved in 1948—

during his study, he found pigeons learned to continue behaviors that coincided with food appearing, despite the food appearing at set intervals. In other words, pigeons saw patterns that produced an outcome they wanted and kept doing it, even though there was no causal relationship.

Shana Wilson from Kent State University investigated why people engage in superstitious behavior. She concluded that people who engage in superstitious behaviors are more susceptible to what is called the *uncertainty-of-outcome hypothesis*, which is the idea that when people feel a lack of certainty, they seek to find a way in which they feel they can exert some degree of control over it. A lack of certainty is extremely uncomfortable and unsettling, and being able to point to something as a cause eases the underlying tension. Certainty is about survival and security and a lack of danger.

Daniel Wann in 2013 discovered that sports fans actually felt that they could influence outcomes of games and matches with their superstitious behaviors, which typically involved clothing, food and drink, and good luck charms. Sports fan or not, the more you feel that your life is determined by factors outside your control, this research would argue, the more likely you'll become superstitious.

Beyond sports fandom, we can see examples of this in our own daily lives. We grow impatient and anxious if we have an acne outbreak, and we are comforted if we find any remedy, no matter how dubious. It makes us feel that we will have things under control, even if the remedy calls for ingredients that make you doubtful. Anything that represents a sliver of hope allows us to feel control versus hopelessness and helplessness.

Not having control over situations, at the extreme end of the spectrum, is a feeling that underlies types of anxiety and depression. What motivation could you possibly have if you were certain everything would turn out terribly, despite your best efforts? Therefore, many times, the more important an uncontrollable situation is, the more likely people are to try to exert a measure of control through superstitious behavior. Some use it as a coping mechanism.

Superstitions are generally harmless, until the point that they are relied upon and replace actual work and effort. Problems arise when people can't distinguish between an outcome they can control and an outcome that is beyond their control. In other words, what is wasted motion to service a superstition and what behaviors are actually impactful? Is the main purpose to reduce anxiety (superstition) or to create progress?

Stuart Vyse, author and professor at Connecticut College, chalks superstitious behaviors up to the comforts of *illusory control*, saying, "There is evidence that positive, luck-enhancing superstitions provide a psychological benefit that can improve skilled performance. There is anxiety associated with the kinds of events that bring out superstition. The absence of control over an important outcome creates anxiety. So, even when we know on a rational level that there is no magic, superstitions can be maintained by their emotional benefit. Furthermore, once you know that a superstition applies, people don't want to tempt fate by not employing it."

Superstitions can generally be split into two categories: positive and negative. A positive superstition sounds like "If I do X, then Y will occur" where Y is a positive outcome. Positive superstitions can improve confidence and reduce anxiety because they are the panacea to all that ails you. They are your lucky charm and best foot forward. If you are shy about a job interview and you always wear lucky socks during job interviews, you are going in with a head full of confidence because you feel you are complete and fully armored for battle.

This provides a psychological advantage and helps us complete the self-fulfilling prophecy where if we think that we are (because of a superstitious behavior, anyway), then we are. They can end up assisting us in life if harnessed and limited properly. Negative superstitions are best characterized as "If X, then no Z" where Z is a negative outcome. This is helpful as well, but it can be a bit more disempowering.

Superstitions are easy to acquire, and they are likely more widespread than you realize. Whenever you are engaging in actions to reduce your anxiety or uncertainty, you might want to ask yourself if you are just servicing a superstitious belief. Doing something "just in case" often ends up doing that. Our brains fool us into a sense of illusory control because it feels more comfortable. However, that comfort sometimes distorts reality in very detrimental ways.

Why Do We Believe in Magic?

Ah, magic—not the type that magicians peddle on sidewalks, but rather the belief in the paranormal and the mystical.

This is something maybe even fewer of us would admit to believing in as adults, but children have been found to accept magic and the paranormal as readily as science. This naturally makes sense because children's brains are sponges for information. They absorb everything and have no sense of perspective on how to separate truth, falsehoods, and the fantastical.

Children accept magic as part of their worldview because they don't understand the world well enough to dispel it. At some point, most people lose their belief in Santa Claus for this very reason. The math doesn't measure up for an obese man whipping a set of flying reindeer across the world, descending through every chimney in the world with gifts and enough time left over to kick his feet up and enjoy a snack of milk and cookies. Many things just don't hold up to increased scrutiny as children grow up and experience more of the world and the boundaries of reality.

Yet we must realize that this doesn't happen to everyone; our sense of magic and the paranormal aren't completely dashed from our lives. There *are* those of us who still believe in Santa Claus and insist on his existence. Generally, Eugene Subbotsky of Lancaster University asserts that the belief in magic persists in the subconscious of many adults even while they consciously reject it.

This means that adults will never admit to it, but they'll secretly hope to catch the obese man dressed in a red suit on their rooftop during Christmas Eve. They feel logically they shouldn't believe in magic and logically they should seek alternate explanations for what they may have heard of or witnessed. They should know better, after all. However, at the slightest hint of unexplained ambiguity, they revert back to what is referred to as "magical thinking"—a self-explanatory term. Adults are more likely to rule out *magic* as an option right off the bat and will instead seek all other alternate explanations before resorting to a paranormal option.

Magical thinking arises in large part for the same reason superstitions take hold in people's minds: being able to blame a boogeyman or credit a savior gives us a sense of control over the world and how we navigate it. If we can blame the rain on a mischievous deity, this is more comforting than a total lack of understanding of rain's origins. It gives us comfort in uncertain times and allows us to remain mentally strong.

This mirrors what we see in everyday life. Adults, for the most part, are conditioned to swear off magical thinking because it can denote a lack of logic, evidence, and even intelligence. Indeed, it is seen as a crutch to simply explain anomalies away as magic, a ghost, or a monster with a hammer. But at a certain point when you find reality difficult to cope with or explain, the brain steps in and concocts something that ties everything together nice and neatly.

Giora Keinan of Tel Aviv University found that those who had the highest levels of magical thinking were also those with the highest levels of stress. It is clear then that magical thinking, whether superstitious or in the belief of salvation, is used as a defense mechanism to protect people's psyches against reality. Indeed, in Israel, citizens were subject to constant missile attacks at the time of the study. The alternative is an enormous level of panic and stress that the brain simply can't function with.

Magical thoughts can make a person feel that they will be okay. If someone's ego is challenged, they will use defense mechanisms to create a scenario in which they are not at fault. Similarly, if someone's sense of logic is challenged, they will use magical thinking to create a scenario in which their thinking is not wrong. Taken to the extreme, magical thinking is seen in delusional breakdowns.

Someone without magical thinking in an extremely dangerous situation will be too beholden to logic to feel okay. They'll calculate the odds of survival or happiness and see that probability is not on their side. Someone with magical thinking can easily thrive in such a position because they possess one of the most important human traits: *hope.* Magical thinking bestows a feeling of hope and that things will turn out all right, and therefore it battles panic.

Jennifer Whitson at the University of Texas conducted additional research into the notion that magical thinking is a type of mental shield from the harsh truths of the world. *If something negative has happened, it was for a reason, or there was a greater purpose behind it.* That's the type of magical thinking that can allow people to mourn more effectively or work through tragedy.

We've established that magical thinking serves to protect us in many ways, but why are there such different levels of acceptance of magical thinking?

Some people frequently get their palms read and avoid black cats like the plague, while others intentionally choose to live on the 13th floor of buildings because they like the number. What accounts for this difference? Research from the University of Helsinki showed that people with greater degrees of magical thinking tended to interpret random moving shapes as being anthropomorphized or having some sort of intent or purpose. Some said the random shapes were playing tag, while people who had low degrees of magical thinking simply saw random shapes moving in tandem. Those with greater degrees of magical thinking also saw hidden faces in photos where no such faces were present.

It seems that people have fundamentally different ways of viewing the world. One group views the world as a puzzle that isn't yet assembled (magical thinkers) while others see it as individual elements (non-magical thinkers).

People with lower degrees of magical thinking seem to be more adept at seeing random data and patterns for what they are, whereas magical thinking is a lens people will look through to interpret their world. A believer in the paranormal will see fate and kismet, where a more skeptical person will see a simple coincidence. A believer in magic will attribute it to unseen forces, where the skeptic will talk about the small world effect. And so on. Rolling with the underlying theme, one group accepts uncertainty while the other does everything within its power to avoid it.

A study from the University of Toulouse concluded that there were indeed certain "cognitive thinking styles" that predicted magical thinking and line up neatly with the other assertions made in this chapter. The researchers delineated two different cognitive thinking styles: intuitive and reflective. Intuitive thinkers go with their gut as quickly as possible, whereas reflective thinkers tend to absorb information and then process it more slowly. In a sense, reflective thinkers are suspicious of their first instincts. Guess which one was more predictive of magical thinking?

Let's take the following scenario: you are walking next to a cemetery at midnight and

71

there is a man in a red leather jacket staggering toward you. He appears to be covered in dirt and mold.

The intuitive thinker will immediately jump to conclusions and come up with the first explanation—clearly a zombie is approaching. This same thought might cross the reflective thinker's mind as well, but they will suppress it in favor of an explanation that takes into account many more factors. This usually results in decidedly *unmagical* thinking.

This isn't to say a belief in magic and the paranormal is negative or unhelpful. It's merely to suggest the genesis of a belief in Santa Claus and the sun being one of the wheels of Apollo's golden chariot arose out of a need for self-defense, feelings of control, and a desire to be significant and purposeful. It wasn't necessarily because people engaged in illogical thought patterns—they were just doing the best they could with the information they possessed.

Just like with superstitions, beliefs in magic and the paranormal can also be positive because they lend confidence to uncertain situations. If someone holds the belief that they fight well in battle during full moons and their next battle happens to fall on a full moon, they will be ready for action.

Superstitions and magic can be seen as flaws in human thinking, but they can also be seen as features in that they act to protect the self. There is no doubt they can occasionally (or often) distort our views of the world, but on the whole, they appear to contribute to mental health and well-being.

Why Do We See Faces in Toast?

With superstitions and magical thinking, you have the symptoms of a brain struggling to feel safe and secure. In doing so, the brain tries to fill in the gaps from the incomplete information it received from the world. We can see the brain's tendency to overcompensate to the point of skewing reality, and perhaps the epitome of this tendency is *pareidolia*: seeing visual patterns in randomness where none exist.

73

Pareidolia, in simpler terms, is seeing an image of Jesus in a piece of toast or picking out formations in clouds as animals. You have probably experienced pareidolia many times, though you may have not realized what your brain was actually doing. The brain is so powerful it is capable of merging information you have stored with incoming signals to find even more patterns; when the brain starts recognizing patterns that are actually just random noise, this is pareidolia.

Pareidolia stems from the fact that as rational beings, we have a desire to make sense of the world. We want things to fit into identifiable categories and for different categories to have clear relationships with one another. In the case of pareidolia, our brains are simply getting confused by the signals it is receiving and identify patterns and correlations that do not exist in an attempt to find understanding.

This can lead us to believe that we have seen things that do not actually exist. For example, consider the life of a Wall Street investor. Investors are notorious for trying to find patterns within the random noise of the stock market. Some use complex algorithms and computer simulations to try to predict the market. Others study the complex information presented in financial reports, and then they try to determine which companies are poised for the biggest gains. Either way, having a good view of the market and stocks is the first step. Then investors must make a decision.

Without quality information and models, the investor would have no idea which stocks were set to increase. This uncertainty would make the investor's job impossible, as investing would become an extremely risky gamble. The investor would likely just throw their hands in the air, fully defeated by their lack of information.

Our brains operate like a stock investor, constantly analyzing our surroundings, building models, and trying to predict the outcomes. This allows us to accurately predict the outcomes of our actions, protect us from known dangers, find nutritious foods, and creates an opening for a wide variety of other behaviors. But just like the stock investor can create a bad model that sees false patterns, so too can our brains find false patterns among all the noise. The fact is, there are not always ghost patterns in what we experience. Some stock investors go bankrupt because they see things that aren't there. Some things are indeed just random chaos.

Perception is an active process within your mind that is constantly trying to incorporate the outside world into familiar mental models. If you close your eyes and imagine a spoon, your ideal model of a spoon will be presented based on your experiences. When you see a spoon you have never seen before, your brain takes this information and incorporates it into your existing model of a spoon.

But what happens when you see an unknown object? Your brain is still going to try to classify the information, so it will compare it to everything it knows. If the object is elongated and metal and has a cupped end, your brain might decide that this is another spoon. In fact, your brain is so adept at this process that it will sometimes ignore or avoid certain aspects of the object to fit it within an existing category. This is like shoving a square peg into a round hole.

One of the most common times pareidolia happens is when our minds try to recognize a face within an inanimate object. This happens all the time. Even the yellow, simplified "smiley face" is a great example. This common symbol has no nose, eyebrows, skin, hair, or any other feature that would let us know it is human. Yet when two black dots are placed above a curved line on a yellow circle, we instantly see a smiling face. This is known as facial pareidolia, and like other forms of pareidolia, it likely has its roots in evolutionary history.

Pareidolia is a subset of a greater phenomenon known as *apophenia,* which is the general process of interpreting false patterns from data. This phenomenon can also happen with information we consume, feelings we have, or even numbers and words that we hear. Recall that pareidolia only occurs when we have found false patterns within the images we see.

Further, pareidolia appears to be largely related to our ability to recognize faces and other objects within our natural environment. For obvious reasons, it has always been important that humans and their ancestors can find food, hide from predators, and recognize their family and friends. Imagine what would have happened to any caveman without these abilities. He would likely be eaten by the first wild animal that he failed to recognize as dangerous. Even if he managed to avoid the wildlife, he would still be lost in a world where he could not tell what tribe he belonged to or who his relatives were.

In fact, famous astronomer and physicist Carl Sagan hypothesized that pareidolia is an overextension of our ability to recognize faces. Sagan succinctly summarized his theory as "Those infants who a million years ago were unable to recognize a face smiled back less, were less likely to win the hearts of their parents, and less likely to prosper."

This ability to recognize a face is a complex process within the brain that analyzes all of the structures and patterns within a human face. Just like your ideal image of a spoon, you have an idealized image of a face. Through trial and error, you learn which of these patterns are faces and which are not. When we interpret a yellow circle with two black dots and a curved line as a face, this is the simplest version of that pattern recognition.

In a sense, we all have a certain degree of facial pareidolia that was necessary for our ancestors to develop bonds and care for each other. As such, people with the ability to discern faces were more likely to survive and more likely to produce offspring. This increased the trait within the human population, and now, like most traits that allowed us to survive in harsh conditions, they are more hindrances than help.

Why Do We See Things That Don't Exist?

The final way in which our brains trick us into chasing ghosts is when we literally see them. Can't blame us for chasing them in that case!

Hallucinations are a brain malfunction in which the sufferer experiences false images or sounds that do not exist in the real world. Hallucinations can be caused by a number of different underlying problems, but they are generally very unpleasant and disorienting for people who experience the malfunction. They're not confined only to seeing a ghost in the dark or hearing a creepy "avenge me" at night; they can come in all tactile sensations that the brain can produce by accident.

For example, a tactile hallucination is when you feel something crawling on your skin, though nothing is there. Sometimes the hallucinations can be simple, such as seeing a pattern of colors obscuring the visual field. Other times they can be immensely complex, such as seeing buildings, people, or even imaginary animals and creatures. The level and type of hallucination depend entirely on what region of the brain is malfunctioning or which signals have been lost to injury or disease.

Hallucinations are not to be confused with an illusion, which is simply the distortion or misinterpretation of real perception. For example, a magician can create the illusion of "levitation" by hiding the wires that lift him off the ground. Without seeing these, the brain wrongly assumes that the magician is levitating through his own power, a common illusion. A hallucination, on the other hand, would be seeing a magician who is not actually there. While some hallucinations can be pleasant, others can often turn dark or scary or generally be disruptive to everyday life.

In general, there are three basic issues that can cause hallucinations. They include (1) diseases of the eye, (2) diseases within the nervous system, and (3) in some cases the use of drugs.

Brain Issues. Whenever the chemistry of the brain is affected in some way, there are changes in patterns of thought and the general way the brain perceives and analyzes the senses. If something disrupts the visual cortex, for example, we can easily misinterpret visual information and our brain will produce a hallucination. We know that there are mechanisms involved that include neurotransmitters and feedback between nerves, but the complexity of the brain makes it hard to pinpoint where a hallucination originates.

There are many brain diseases that include hallucinations as symptoms. Schizophrenia and delirium are both highly associated with hallucinations. Schizophrenics often experience auditory hallucinations, such as a voice that seems to be coming from outside their body. Many other brain diseases also cause hallucinations, likely because the normal audio or visual systems are interrupted and the brain must fill in the gaps somewhere. Delirium is another mental illness that often leads to hallucinations and a variety of other symptoms. Delirium can be caused by everything from high fever to alcohol withdrawal, yet a third of all people with delirium will experience visual hallucinations.

Strokes and other injuries that cause brain damage are also highly associated with hallucinations, in part because they change the very nerves that must process and deal with external signals. When a stroke happens in the occipital lobe, the hallucinations will likely be visual, as this area is usually used to process visual cues. If the damage happens within the temporal lobes, auditory hallucinations are more common because these areas are largely in control of auditory processing.

People with severe migraines often experience "Alice-in-Wonderland" syndrome, a type of visual hallucination in which objects are distorted, gaining or losing size as the patient views them. In fact, part of the masterpiece behind Carroll's story is Alice's constantly changing perspectives. Modern doctors would likely diagnose Alice as having severe hallucinations.

Many people experience hypnagogic (sleep-inducing) or hypnopompic (exiting sleep) hallucinations that occur as their minds slip into or out of reality while they sleep. Further, seizures are largely related to hallucinations, in part because they change the chemistry and processing within various regions of the brain. Many seizure patients have reported olfactory hallucinations, such as bad smells, likely indicating that there is some damage within the olfactory lobes of the brain.

Drug-Induced Hallucinations. While we don't understand all of the mechanisms behind drug-induced hallucinations, humans have been using a number of plants, fungi, and animal derivatives to induce hallucinations throughout history.

There are many street drugs that cause hallucinations, in part because they stimulate or reduce activity in various regions of the brain. These drugs include

LSD and PCP, though there are many legal medicines that have hallucinations as an adverse side effect. Many of these drugs regulate or control various chemicals that nerves use to communicate. Interrupting these signals can lead to many types of hallucination, from visual to olfactory. Interestingly, some of the drugs designed for Parkinson's disease affect the dopaminergic network, which in effect causes hallucinations in some patients.

Psychedelic drugs typically work by affecting receptors in your brain that alter the way the nerves communicate with each other. When stimulated by drugs, certain regions of your brain start firing more than normal and can lead to the end user experiencing patterns, colors, or even full-blown visual hallucinations like objects, animals, or people. Research has suggested that hallucinations are largely caused by interactions they have within the brain's cortex, which is the area that processes incoming signals. Many of these drugs activate 5-HT2A receptors, which are normally triggered by natural chemicals within the brain. In fact, some hallucinations are caused because the receptors are not just turned "off" or "on" but are put into a completely different mode of activation that the brain is not used to. This likely causes the hallucinogenic effects of many drugs, as your brain tries to put a reality to its new internal mechanisms.

Eye Issues. Humans are very visual creatures, and our brains have developed complex pathways for interpreting the signals we receive from our eyes. In fact, it is thought that hallucinations are only slightly different than visualization, which is the ability to see images within your mind. When your eyes become damaged due to disease or an accident, your brain sometimes overcompensates for the lack of information and starts filling in the gaps with hallucinations. This been documented in many eye diseases such as macular degeneration.

A common disease with hallucinations is Charles Bonnet syndrome, named for a man who suffered hallucinations after being blinded in both eyes by cataracts. Charles Bonnet syndrome is a form of hallucinating that is caused specifically by the loss of visual signals. Typically, these forms of hallucinations will only be visual, as there is still input from the ears. Without the input from the eyes, the brain fills in the missing information with a "best guess" with previous images.

This syndrome has also been found in other eye diseases, such as macular degeneration. In fact, our brains are so good at hallucinating that anyone can try this at home. Simply tape two ping pong ball halves over your eyes so they can still open but you can see no images. After only a few hours in this condition, many people start to hallucinate visual objects, color, or even people.

In fact, psychologists have studied this phenomenon in the lab. By placing 19 healthy volunteers in a sensory-deprivation room, they were able to determine that it only takes around 15 minutes of deprivation for most people to start hallucinating sounds, images, and tactile sensations. Not only this, but most of the volunteers felt a depressed mood or paranoia. This supports the conclusion that our brains rely on sensory information not only to build a picture of reality but also that the sensory information itself is helping us maintain a happy and healthy mind.

This is further evidence that hallucinations are an extension of the brain's ability to visualize, only the visualization replaces the absent sensory signals, such as eyesight. Researchers call this ability "faulty source monitoring," as the brain forgets where the signal came from and thus believes that the visualization came from outside of the body.

Psychologist Oliver Mason of the University College London summed up the situation in this way: "Basically, something that actually is initiated within us gets misidentified as [being] from the outside."

This seems to show that hallucinations in and of themselves are not a disease but simply the symptom of losing access to a sensory signal. The separation between visualization and hallucination is a fine line that is normally separated by the reality of information we are receiving through our eyes. Without that information, visualizations can become stronger and eventually the brain replaces the lost signals with creations of its own. For example, people have also experienced sound hallucinations after losing their hearing, as the brain malfunctions in a similar way and tries to replace the lost signal.

Takeaways:

- We see things that don't exist, we do things that don't make a difference, and we believe in things that are fantasy. Why? Don't we know better? As always, the logical answer is yes, but as humans, we are not ruled by sense of logic and rationality. *It just feels better sometimes.* A dog probably knows he shouldn't ruin his owner's new shoes, but sometimes he just can't help it. Yes, I just compared us to dogs.

- We can't help but be a little bit superstitious. This is when we feel that an illusory cause-and-effect relationship exists. This can be caused by any number of things such as conditioning. It gives us a sense of control and certainty about the world and thus the feeling that we can affect outcomes for ourselves. This may not be true, but it's a comforting and secure feeling versus feeling that we are at the mercy of the universe's randomness.
- We can't help but have some magical thoughts. This provides a sense of certainty in that we are able to process and understand the unexplainable—even if it is incorrect. For some of us, magical thinking arises because we are rather intuitive thinkers versus reflective thinkers—intuitive thinkers go with their gut reaction and make connections and assumptions more naturally.
- We can't help but see faces in toast, butter, and clouds. Why is that? Because of pareidolia, which is the human tendency to see patterns, especially

faces, in random static noise. We see them because they help us survive and thrive—quicker pattern recognition led to quicker hunting, killing, and thinking. Now that we don't need to think in those terms most of the time, pareidolia still occurs because we are always trying to make sense of the world by comparing it to old knowledge we possess and seeing what preexisting models it might fit.

- We can't help but see things that don't exist. Some of us have hallucinations from time to time, and they stem from three causes generally: brain problems, drugs, or visual problems. They are not features of a healthy brain, and they can occur in just about any form you can imagine. Here we are literally chasing ghosts—apparitions that don't exist.

Chapter 4. Faulty Memories

Although we don't like to admit it, sometimes our memories are flat-out wrong.

For instance, suppose you are in a fight with your significant other about whose turn it is to wash the dishes. You feel that your memory is a steel trap and you did the dishes for the past week, so obviously it is their turn. Yet they swear the same thing. Whose memory is inaccurate, and how can you even begin to determine that?

Obviously one party's memory is incorrect, or both of them are. And yet there is such confidence that each person's representation of the past is true and unflawed. What's happening when a small conflict like this occurs? Is someone trying to maliciously lie or bend reality to suit their own needs? What about when this happens with larger consequences, such as with testimony in a lawsuit? It wouldn't be inaccurate to say that our existences are the sum of our memories, and yet they can be so fragile, fickle, and outright inaccurate.

In most cases, this is due to a malfunctioning of our memory systems. What else might be affected by these errors besides the dishes? A lot! You would be right to question some of the bigger events of your life and if they happened the way you think they did.

Our memories are an unreliable narrator at best, and even if they remember the concrete, black and white events, they will inevitably be altered by our individual perspectives and biases. For instance, you may feel that you've done the dishes for 10 days in a row, but in actuality you only feel that way because there is a long history of squabbling over household chores. Our memory is its own editor and director of photography and will create its own version of reality. It gets us into trouble, causes misunderstandings, and makes us doubt ourselves. It *works for us*, and this is a distinctly different function than being *accurate*.

It's beneficial to first take a quick look at the structure of memory and how it works before discussing the design flaws. Memory is how we store and retrieve information for use, and there are three steps to creating a memory. An error in any of these steps will result in information that is not effectively converted to memory—a weak memory or the feeling of "I can't remember his name, but he was wearing purple..." The three steps are as follows:

1. Encoding
2. Storage
3. Retrieval

Encoding is the step of experiencing information through your senses. We do this constantly, and you are doing it right now. We encode information both consciously and subconsciously through all of our senses. If you are reading a book, you are using your eyes to encode information. The more attention and focus you devote to an activity, the more conscious and deep your encoding becomes. This gives information the best chance to continue along the path to becoming a memory and consequently whether that information stops at short-term memory or makes it all the way to long-term memory. However, over longer periods of time, we are even able to subconsciously encode information into long-term memory.

Storage is the next step after you've experienced information with your senses and encoded it. What happens to the information once it passes through your eyes or ears? The information goes to a processing center that determines what happens to it—its path is determined by how deeply encoded it was through focus, repetition, or practice. There are three choices for where this information can go, and they determine whether it's a traditional memory—a piece of information that you consciously know—or something you won't remember the next day or even hour.

There are three places the information can end up, and thus we can say there are three memory systems: sensory memory, short-term memory, and long-term memory. **Sensory memory** is the first level of memory, and it stores information for only an instant and as long as it is important. This is how a piece of sand feels to sit on. **Short-term memory** is what we're most familiar with, and it can retain "seven plus or minus two" pieces of information for roughly 20 seconds on average. This is the phone number of a restaurant you are researching for dinner. **Long-term memory** is where memories become a real, physical manifestation as a result of neurons making connections. This is your home address or social security number.

The last step of the memory process is **retrieval**, which is the act of recalling information or remembering it. This is when a piece of information is actually useful—when it can be recalled at a later point either consciously or unconsciously. Again, how easily you can retrieve it depends on how deeply the information was encoded in the first place and which memory system it ended up in.

If the information was deeply encoded, you might be able to recall it from nothing. If it was something you should have rehearsed a bit more, you might need a cue or reminder to call up the information. Most memory isn't necessarily focused on retrieval—it's focused on the storage aspect and what you can do to shoehorn memories from sensory and short-term areas into long-term areas or at least retain information long enough so we can pass a test or secure a promotion.

Memory may seem relatively simple, but there are many moving parts and at least three steps where the process can go wrong—and that's with me skipping most of the minutiae. All of this adds up to tell us exactly how inaccurate and faulty our recollections can be. You may have what you think is your true view of the world, and it can be disconcerting to realize that what you think you know is completely inaccurate.

Even a relatively minor phenomena you've probably dealt with known as *tip of the tongue* (TOT) is an insight into the complexity of memory. This occurs when you know what you wanted to say but your mind suddenly runs blank or when you walk into a room and realize you have no idea why you did so. We might confidently feel that we know something but come up empty when we seek to recall specific details. It probably occurs to me on a daily basis.

Psychologist William James first coined the term TOT in 1890: "A sort of wraith of the name is in it, beckoning us in a given direction, making us at moments tingle with the sense of our closeness and then letting us sink back without the longed-for term."

For the next few decades, it was noted as a peculiar trait of memory. It wasn't until 1966 that researchers from Harvard

University studied why knowledge appears to be at our fingertips and yet so far away. In the 1966 study, researchers read aloud word definitions to participants and then asked them to recall the defined words. They found that there was a very specific set of behaviors they engaged in if they were in a TOT state—they could remember what the word was and perhaps even what it meant. They could also provide synonyms for it and words that rhymed with it. However, they were still not always able to recall the exact defined word.

If this feeling feels like torture to you, it's because the researchers accurately characterize it as the feeling of *imminent recall*. If we keep hunting around for it, we might find it. We might also never come up with the trigger for it, despite ruminating for hours or days. The sensation of knowing that you know something yet don't know it at the moment is supremely frustrating. It's like being on the verge of a satisfying sneeze for hours.

A study from McMaster University has posited that the TOT phenomenon occurs because specific words get lost in translation from the brain to the mouth. The brain translates a thought or memory from an abstract, intangible concept into a word, and then the word is sent to our sensory systems to make the proper sound. This is the process of expressing anything via speaking, and it's far more complex than we give it credit for. This means information stored as a memory is now also subject to the moving parts of the language expression system.

The McMaster researchers put participants into TOT states by asking, "What do you call the sport of exploring caves?" This is something the participants vaguely knew but were typically unable to correctly recall. They were given time to think, and if they didn't produce the word, the researchers provided them with the answer. Days or weeks later, the participants were asked the same question and were shown to exhibit the same TOT states. They pointed to this as proof that TOT behavior is something that can be reinforced, just like a memory. In other words, if you make the same error and fall into a TOT state, you are likely to do it again with that same word.

Other hypotheses about the TOT effect are that the brain has limited capacity, and anything that isn't immediately rehearsed or introduced into long-term memory exists in a hazy, cloudy region where TOT is just a byproduct. You might know that you know the information, but you may have neglected to rehearse sufficiently to actually be able to recall it without a strong clue, such as "The color rhymes with *blorange*." Essentially, this is a failure in memory encoding or memory retrieval. With memory encoding, the information simply may not be there, while with memory retrieval, the information is there, but there may be too many distractions or barriers for you to effectively recall it. All this complexity for a simple TOT? Let's go deeper.

Déjà Vu: "This Feels Familiar…"

Déjà vu, the sense of "I know I've experienced this before..." is still a mystery to scientists. There are multiple theories about what is actually happening in our memory banks for us to feel familiarity in a new or novel situation, but none has gained a consensus. It occurs when we encounter an event or image that feels very familiar, like it's not the first time we've been there—yet we are unable to recall from where, and it may indeed be the first encounter. It seems like our memories are fabricating experiences for us or, alternatively, creating false feelings of familiarity for an unknown reason.

This eerie intuition happens to between 60% and 70% of us, most of whom are between the ages of 15 and 25 years old. Due to it being a miswiring of the brain, you might suppose that it occurs more to the elderly—it doesn't, so that almost adds to the mystery. Is it something that only happens when the brain is developing and pruning down its mistakes? More mystery abounds.

Déjà vu is the French expression meaning "already seen." Because déjà vu happens so randomly and in people without a clear medical condition to explain it away, it is a difficult phenomenon to study. Even the why and how of the phenomenon is up for debate. Psychoanalysts—in the vein of Sigmund Freud and unfulfilled unconscious drivers—tend to believe it is wishful thinking and an overly active subconscious, while psychiatrists—in the vein of exorcising past traumas—often attribute the experience to the brain mistaking the present for the past.

Perhaps the simplest and most plausible explanation is that déjà vu is a result of wayward memories that were once learned but forgotten, leading to feelings of familiarity despite no real recollection. Imagine receiving a light burn scar on your hand that fades over time to the point where you forget it happened, though there remains a small discolored mark. While a leading idea, it doesn't quite explain the results that many scientists have produced in their research on déjà vu. All of the evidence points to déjà vu being more of a biological phenomenon in our hippocampus, the brain structure where the memory resides.

One leading theory is that déjà vu is an error in the way we process memories. When we process information from our daily lives, our brains go through a specific sequence. (1) First, our brains search through our memories to see if we can gain understanding through comparison to a past experience, and if it comes up with a match, (2) a separate area of the brain identifies the new situation as familiar, and context is instantly gained. This helps with quick processing and analysis of novel situations. For instance, we may never have driven a motorcycle before, but our brains can compare it ever so slightly to aspects of riding a bicycle.

During an episode of déjà vu, the second part of the process seems to be triggered by accident. This is when you see something that isn't related to a bicycle, but that feeling arises anyway.

For a more illustrative example from the other side, if you find yourself in line at a café and standing behind a clown making balloons while balancing on a unicycle (something you are sure to be unfamiliar with), a déjà vu moment would result in you identifying this situation as familiar and not novel. This occurs unconsciously, but consciously, you will be hit with opposing feelings of familiarity and novelty. That ensuing confusion is what we are most familiar with.

For a third theory, déjà vu is theorized to be a miscommunication between sensory input and our memories recalled. Some researchers speculate that the brain, in an attempt to make sense of the world with the limited amount of information we are actually able to process, fills in the gaps of the information that is missing. For our brains, it only takes a small amount of sensory information to have us recall detailed information. Taking our clown café example from earlier, this theory would suggest that our brains create a feeling of déjà vu because there are individual elements that are similar to what we have experienced in the past. Overall, déjà vu helps provide a more complete picture of what is happening, though it may not be accurate or warranted.

A similar idea states that déjà vu is simply a timing error—as we take in a moment with our senses, the data is being stored in long-term and short-term storage at the same time. Two processes occurring at the same time clutters up our mental bandwidth and causes a delay between the moment and storing it, which we may experience as that unsettling feeling of déjà vu.

Finally, déjà vu might be a sign of the brain checking its memory for integrity and slip-ups. This theory comes from researcher Akira O'Connor and was created after he noticed brain areas involving decision-making (the prefrontal cortex) as opposed to memory (the hippocampus) become active during induced déjà vu. To

O'Connor, this implied that the brain is actively thinking through memories and then sending signals if there is a mismatch between the memory and what actually happened.

Of the multiple potential causes for déjà vu, Dr. Elizabeth Reichelt of the University of New South Wales has said the following:

> So far there is no simple explanation as to why Déjà Vu occurs. It is thought that Déjà Vu could be evoked by a mismatch between the sensory input and memory-recalling output. This theory indicates that the mismatch between knowing an event is new, but it feeling familiar is because of sensory environmental information going straight into long term memory… The familiarity we

experience in a Déjà Vu event exposes that there are different memory systems located in the hippocampus. Instead of sensory environmental information passing from short-term stores into long-term memory, in Déjà Vu, information bypasses short-term memory and instead reaches long-term memory stores directly. This explains why a new experience can feel familiar, but not as tangible as a fully recalled memory.

As to why our brains have this processing quirk, it has been asserted that human memory developed this ability to help survival. The ability to recognize new situations and predict the future based on past experiences may have helped us avoid certain dangers. It's safer and more thorough than depending merely on your actual memories, which are necessarily limited. For instance, if you were walking into a dark alley and you had a sudden déjà vu feeling of a past bad experience, you might be safer.

One thing is certain—it's an odd feeling that makes us doubt our reality. One peculiar aspect of this is the notion that déjà vu makes us feel like we can predict the future. Suppose you're doing something that feels so familiar that you know what will happen next. That's just a natural direction for your thoughts to go. This is known as *precognition*. Are precognition and déjà vu two sides of the same coin? Or is it more likely that experiencing one simply makes experiencing the other more likely?

Anne Cleary, a cognitive psychologist at Colorado State University, has dispelled this misplaced belief and shown that the feeling of knowledge that déjà vu can sometimes impart is only a feeling. She did so by having participants watch video scenes in which they went through a series of turns. Déjà vu was then induced, and they were asked what the final turn in the video would be. They mostly guessed wrong, although they felt confident that they could predict the future.

In the end, déjà vu ends up being one of the more mysterious quirks of memory because of how the scientific community still collectively shrugs at the cause. However, it may pale in comparison to the next memory malfunction: false and implanted memories.

False Memories: "I Swear It Wasn't Me."

> Perhaps what we actually remember is a set of memory fragments stitched onto a fabric of our own devising. If we sew cleverly enough, we have made ourselves a memorable story easy to recall. – Carl Sagan

False memories are on the extreme end of the spectrum, where it's not a matter of remembering incorrectly or forgetting a few details—it's about starting with a narrative or emotion and making your memories fit instead of the other way around through observing the world and recording what you see. This is where we start with a conclusion in mind and bend our memories to fit it. We mentioned earlier that our memory's purpose is not exactly to record reality; it's to reinforce whatever conclusion or feelings we wanted reinforced. It's there for our benefit, not our analysis.

A 2014 study published in the *Journal of Neuroscience* studied how our brains rewrite our memories to be more useful and helpful. In the study, people looked at objects with backgrounds on a computer screen. Then they had to place the object in the original location but on a new background. The participants always put the object in the wrong spot. Finally, they were shown the object in three locations—where it was originally, where it had been placed the second time, and a brand-new location—and asked to pick the correct spot for it. The researchers found that people always chose the second location rather than the first. Their memories were literally updated with more accurate information; this can be seen as a survival mechanism for better decision-making. It's also a scary peek into how susceptible our memories are to after-the-fact editing to fit a narrative or purpose.

Just because our memories are capable of remarkable feats doesn't mean that they aren't subject to errors that are just as remarkable. False memories are a topic that has been heavily explored in neuroscience, with no real conclusion other than "they happen because our memories are gullible."

A false memory is a memory that is neurologically identical to a real memory but based on something that did not actually happen.

In 1995, Elizabeth Loftus and Jim Coan from the University of California, Irvine, conducted a study to investigate how to implant a false memory by fusing it with an existing, real memory. The study involved a subject who was given descriptions of three true memories from his childhood and one false memory. The subject wrote about each of the four memories for five days in a row, giving a summary and any details or facts he could remember about each of the memories (again, three real and one false).

Over the five days, the subject began to recall more and more about the false memory, introducing details that were never there and that seemed to stem completely from the subject's imagination. He purported to remember everyone that was present and even the emotions involved. He was adding onto the false memory, not realizing that he was treating it as a real memory, and quickly blurring the lines even though he was aware it was made up. At the end, the descriptions were all equally detailed and legitimate-sounding.

Weeks later, the subject was asked to rate his memories for how clear they were. He gave the false memory the second highest rating out of the four memories presented. He could provide vivid detail—perhaps because it was fabricated, so the details conformed to his idea of what the experience would usually entail. And just like that, he wasn't sure which parts had really transpired or not. He may have known that the memory as a whole was false, but he couldn't determine how much of it was made up anymore. Memories could be implanted in people just by saying that they had occurred a few times.

Are we really so accepting? Well, yes. Memories, if they are not entirely false or fabricated, can also be influenced by things as small as suggestive word choice, phrasing, and vocabulary. Another study conducted in 1974 by Loftus at the University of California, Irvine, illustrates this effect.

Subjects watched different videos of car accidents at three different speeds. After, they filled out a survey that asked, "About how fast were the cars going when they *smashed* into each other?"

Other groups of subjects watched the exact same videos and filled out a survey after as well, but the survey instead asked, "About how fast were the cars going when they *bumped/hit/contacted* each other?" The estimates the subjects gave changed in relation to the verb used, which influenced the perception of speed and impact.

- Smashed = 40.8 mph
- Bumped = 38.1 mph
- Hit = 34 mph
- Contacted = 31.8 mph

This simple change in vocabulary affected people's perception of an event and, in essence, changed their memory surrounding it. How reliable can memory truly be when we are manipulated by such small variables? This was an event that the subjects watched on video—and the speed increased by nearly 10 mph when leading language was used—a discrepancy of 25%.

There are no real *biological* explanations for these things, as the three-step process to creating a memory is the same with fake or real information—the brain processes it all the same. So what tendency underlies our gullibility? It's more of a *psychological* tendency; perhaps it is our drive to protect our egos and shield ourselves from judgment or being wrong.

Sometimes, despite our best efforts, however, we are indeed wrong! This is courtesy of what's known as the *Mandela effect*, named for the phenomena of countless people falsely remembering that Nelson Mandela died in prison in the 1980s, when in fact he only died a few years ago in 2013. At first, this was "explained" as a manifestation of movement between parallel universes, each with their own different set of world history events. That explanation, however, is somewhat less likely than simple confusion and fabrication of memories through social reinforcement. In other words, if one person says something, you might believe it, but this belief grows stronger the more you hear it.

The ease with which false memories are created is why eyewitness testimony occupies such an ambivalent place in the legal system. Memories can change each time a witness is interviewed, and sometimes they can be intentionally manipulated by one or both parties. For example, Annalies Vredeveldt of the University of Amsterdam states that asking questions about a memory can easily take a wrong turn if you ask questions as simple as, "What was the color of his hair?" or "He was a redhead, wasn't he?" The first question assumes that there was a male, and the second question assumes that there was a redheaded male. Both questions are leading and draw their own conclusions. As we saw earlier with the choice of vocabulary changing people's estimations of speed, a direct implication can have even more powerful effects on a memory.

Eyewitness accounts are highly trusted by juries yet highly condemned by judges and attorneys who know better. Researcher Julia Shaw states that to implant a false memory, "you try to get someone to confuse their imagination with their memory and get them to repeatedly picture it happening."

This means simply repeating a false memory or story to someone can cause them to confuse the false memory with reality and eventually mesh them together with the real account. There is a very thin and blurry line between memory and imagination, and we saw it in action with one of Loftus's earlier studies.

Eyewitness testimony has been questioned since Hugo Munsterberg's seminal 1908 book *On the Witness Stand*. He questioned the reliability of memory and perception, and the legal community has taken notice ever since. What's scary is that research has shown that juries can't tell the difference between false and accurate witness testimony and often simply rely on how confident the eyewitness is (Nicholson, 2014).

As we will soon learn with flashbulb memories, confidence is never the hallmark of accuracy. Additional support for the distrust in eyewitness testimony has been found in analyses by Scheck and Neufel, who proved that eyewitness testimony was frequently present in cases of suspects who were later exonerated based on DNA evidence.

With the knowledge of how unreliable memory can be and just how easy it is to implant false or biased memories, it's a wonder eyewitness testimony is still allowed at all. Christopher French of the University of London sums it up best: "There is currently no way to distinguish, in the absence of independent evidence, whether a particular memory is true or false. Even memories which are detailed and vivid and held with 100 percent conviction can be completely false."

Our memories are incredible, but the same malleability that leads to memory feats can also be exploited to show great flaws. These create flawed thinking, not out of unsound logic or perception, but if you literally remember something to be different from reality, you're going to have some kind of trouble. The main goal of our brains isn't to be accurate or even helpful, and thus, it can be easily manipulated and tricked.

Flashbulb Memories: "Do You Remember Where You Were During 9/11?"

One curious and constant aspect of memories is just how confident we are in them, despite how malleable they are. We've explored this in previous sections, but this disparity of confidence and accuracy is the most glaring when we talk about *flashbulb memories*.

A flashbulb memory is a memory that feels like you can reach out and touch it. It is incredibly vivid, clear, and detailed. It creates an almost supernatural sense of knowledge where you feel that everything is burned into your brain for the rest of your life. For example, depending on your age, do you remember where you were and what you were doing the moment you heard or read about the tragedy of 9/11 or the assassination of President John F. Kennedy? It can also be a personal event, such as finding out that you are pregnant. Though the term was coined later, this phenomenon has existed since large events like the assassination of President Abraham Lincoln and the bombing of Pearl Harbor.

I remember watching the attack on the World Trade Center on television at school and hearing the school announcements while in a daze in my biology class. The voice on the intercom was close to tears, and the rest of the people in the classroom were sitting in stunned silence. The professor wasn't present at the time, but I remember that the person sitting next to me gasped and grabbed her blue sweater tightly. I was wearing black Nike sneakers, and halfway through, the professor walked into the classroom. At least, that's what I *think* I recall.

Flashbulb memories are built around significant and life-changing events, whether personal or historical. As such, there was a large emotional impact on you, and this intense flash of emotion makes you feel like you remember everything about that exact moment. This just might be the origin of why near-death experiences are like seeing your life flash before your eyes.

In either case, you are put into a reaction of awe and shock. Biologically, this means your senses are alert and adrenaline is coursing through your body. You might be shaking afterward because of the excess adrenaline.

Your heart might be beating fast, and your palms might be sweaty. Because of the emotional impact, flashbulb memories have been seen to involve the amygdala, one of the brain's main processing centers for emotion.

All of this adds up to a belief that you know exactly what is happening at that moment. This might be true, but whether you remember it accurately or not is a different matter.

The term "flashbulb memories" was coined in 1977 by Roger Brown and James Kulik, who proposed that they existed and were forever etched into our brains as an evolutionary defense mechanism. Suppose you were attacked by a wild animal, something that would cause a flashbulb memory because it is so emotionally traumatic and impactful. Brown and Kulik hypothesized that the use of flashbulb memories was so we can go back in time, to the moment of danger, and analyze in great detail how we can avoid similar situations in the future.

Strong emotional impact is the genesis of a flashbulb memory. Therefore, whether flashbulb memories are formed is largely subjective. Flashbulb memories are intense, but they have been shown to be less than reliable. As you've read in this book, our memories are highly susceptible to manipulation, whether they get mixed up with fantasy or daydream, they degrade naturally, are skewed by our natural biases, or are influenced by other factors.

For example, if you develop a flashbulb memory around 9/11, your account could shift according to the following:

- How you daydreamed about making an impromptu patriotic speech in front of your family.
- What your friends told you about 9/11 and their flashbulb memories surrounding it.
- How you feel about 9/11 and your reaction.

Let's also address what happens to us when we are in a physiological state of high arousal. Imagine when you are angry or emotional. Is this typically when we see things objectively or accurately? Is this when reality is the clearest to us and when we can think with the most clarity? In fact, it's the opposite. The very conditions that make us susceptible to creating flashbulb memories are the ones that make them inaccurate.

We emphasize this because much of the research surrounding flashbulb memories is about their accuracy. People's confidence in them has historically been high. On September 12, 2001, David Rubin and Jennifer Talarico, researchers from

Lafayette College, asked a group of students about their memories regarding the attacks the day prior. They also asked them questions about the week prior to the attacks. This allowed them to directly compare a flashbulb memory and a normal memory of life and see how their accuracy kept up over time. Of course, the memories about 9/11 were far more vivid and confident.

After one week, both memories had about the same rate of accuracy and consistency. But at separate points of one month, and seven months after September 12, the rate of inaccuracy and forgetting was also the same between the two memories. In addition, there was the same rate of errors introduced. In the end, flashbulb and normal memories ended up having the same accuracy. There was nothing special about them in the one way that memories are measured in: accuracy.

It's a scary thought to believe in something so much and yet still have it be proven incorrect. The only thing that truly separates flashbulb memories from normal memories is our perception of them.

Overall, they continue to emphasize how suggestible our brains are. Memories are unremarkable and common—what's to stop them from being easily confused, mixed up, or entirely planted and fabricated? Unfortunately, nothing. Recall that our realities are the sum of our memories—so what does that mean if we want to understand the simple difference between objective accuracy and subjective perspective? I'll be waiting for the answer.

Takeaways:

- Our brains have been proven quite imperfect thus far, and perhaps the best demonstration of this is how our memories work: poorly. Our realities are only a collection of our memories, so this is troubling. This starts from the process of creating a memory from scratch and how many steps can go wrong in that process of encoding, storing, and retrieving. But it doesn't end there.

- Next, we try to decipher the mystery of déjà vu, which is when you find yourself in a novel or foreign situation only to feel that you've been there before. There are multiple explanations for this, ranging from a memory-encoding error to a simple forgotten exposure or a miscommunication in the brain's different memory systems. What is the real cause? We can't say yet for certain, but we can say that it doesn't allow us the gift of precognition, as some have theorized.
- False and implanted memories are another problem. You might assume that the only ways our memories can change are due to the passage of time. Unfortunately, our memories are simply not set in stone. They are incredibly malleable and flawed and can't easily distinguish what happened in reality. Thus, it is easy to create false memories and it becomes difficult to find the accurate perspective.
- Finally, the more confident we are in our memories, the less accurate they tend to be. This is shown with flashbulb

memories, which are moments of time that seem to be vivid in detail and usually spurred on by an emotional impact. The problem is that when we are emotional, we are prone to thinking in ways that are anything but clear, measured, and accurate. Even though we feel like these flashbulb memories are untouchable, they decay at the same rate as normal memories.

Chapter 5. SOLD!

How often have you gone to the grocery store and come home with a bunch of items you hadn't planned on buying and hadn't even wanted? You went with the intention of simply buying black pepper for your dinner, but *something* about the advertisements in the store made it impossible for you to abstain. Once you empty your shopping bags at home, you instantly regret your purchases because you don't actually have a use for five pounds of broccoli and two jars of peanut butter—you're even slightly allergic to peanuts! Yet somehow, you picked them up, they made it into your shopping cart, and you didn't object when the cashier rang them up.

When was the last time you bought something you won't use, and will never use, just because it seemed like a good idea at the store? You may have been seduced by the big LIMITED-TIME DISCOUNT sign or the endorsement of thousands of dentists. Whatever the case, these products additionally promise to enrich your life and solve all of your problems. Shockingly, those things didn't happen, but it's okay; there will be a product next week that just might do the same thing.

One of the most glaring examples of how our brains malfunction on a daily and casual basis is in regards to how and why we spend our money. This is all about *the psychology of buying and being sold*. Left to ourselves, our buying tendencies might actually be smart and beneficial in some cases. But actually, this is something that's being constantly done *to* us to accentuate those tendencies and fool us into questionable decisions. It's been happening for decades and has only gotten more sophisticated in the age of technology.

The reality is that clever advertisers have come up with a plethora of ways to part us from our hard-earned cash. In a way, they are the masters of creating poor judgment and making you commit thinking errors. You might think you know some of the obvious ones, such as seeing "limited time only, so buy now" or "9/10 dentists recommend our product over others," but that's just the tip of the iceberg. Advertisers' techniques create the psychological impulse to act or buy in countless ways.

They know exactly how to capture your attention and what buttons to push to make you open your wallet over and over again. Surprisingly, the way to induce this tendency is wholly unrelated to the shiny colors of billboards or even the pricing itself. Those are the surface-level aspects that merely get your attention but may not trigger the buying impulse. What makes us spend money goes much deeper and taps into the core of what motivates us as human beings. We're not psychologically programmed to give more than we want, but we *are* programmed to satisfy our inner desires.

What follows in this chapter is an examination of some of the most common ways we are psychologically triggered into buying. We'll start with psychology professor Robert Cialdini's infamous six keys to persuasion, then talk about gamification and how a sense of progress and achievement motivates sales, delve into how appealing to fear can be extremely powerful, and finally discuss the science of celebrity endorsements. Hopefully you can begin to notice these popping up in your everyday life and save yourself a few dollars in the process.

Six Weapons of Mass Influence

There is perhaps no better demonstration for the separation of how we wish to act versus how we are subconsciously influenced to act than Robert Cialdini's methods, discussed in his seminal 1984 book *Influence: The Psychology of Persuasion.*

Cialdini discussed six weapons of mass influence that underlie many of our actions and subtly persuade us in a certain direction. The book in general stemmed from his desire to understand the techniques of salespeople and how they were able to persuade people to act against their best interests and purchase things they didn't need. In truth, these six weapons touch on fundamental human needs, desires, and predispositions and can be applied far more widely than just in advertising or sales.

For instance, if you want to convince a friend of yours to meet at a certain restaurant, you might say something like "There are 500 reviews and they are all amazing." This is related to one of Cialdini's six principles and it is something we do naturally, which further demonstrates how much of basic human psychology that he was able to identify and articulate.

His influence factors are listed below:

1. Social proof

2. Liking
3. Reciprocation
4. Scarcity
5. Authority
6. Commitment

We'll go through each of them individually, and you will begin to understand just how widespread they are and how big of an impact they have on you without your conscious awareness. It's rare to see an advertisement that *doesn't* invoke at least one of these six methods.

Social proof is taking a cue from other people to make our decisions. If we observe others leaning a certain way, then we will as well because "if so many people are doing it, they can't be wrong," even though they clearly can be. You can also think of this as the mob mentality at work. We feel safe following the lead of others—the more people involved, the safer we feel that we are making a wise decision, even one that we might regret skipping over. When we follow others, we are able to expend less brainpower and ultimately claim less accountability for our actions because we can just blame someone else. It's just an easy way to outsource decision-making, especially if you tend to be indecisive or uncertain—you can just go the way of the majority.

This is why testimonials and reviews play such a heavy part in persuading someone to make a certain decision. Monkey see, monkey do. "Millions of people just like you agree!" Advertisers force you to open your wallet by proclaiming that their product has the consensus agreement, and in most cases, we will use that as a proxy for quality, value, and overall worth. Social proof causes money to be spent because, most of the time, we just want something that has a high chance of being good and a low chance of being bad. Our money goes where *most* people seem to spend it.

Liking takes something you've subconsciously known your whole life and makes it an official aspect of the psychology of buying. We are more easily persuaded and influenced by people we like, people we find attractive, people who appear to be more similar to us, and people who seem to like us in return.

We feel that they have our best interests at heart and that we can trust them more. Furthermore, if they are more similar to us, then we feel that they innately understand us and have the same worldview as us. You'd probably listen to someone from your remote, tiny high school more than someone who is from another country based solely on their perceived similarity and trust. We will buy more easily from people who we have a rapport with, which is why salesmen typically spend so much time nurturing relationships, buttering you up, and complimenting your ugly golf swing—they are in it for the long-term sale, which banks on likability.

A study conducted between business graduate students saw that when the students were told to negotiate as they normally would, there was a 55% chance of coming to an amicable agreement. However, students in a second group were told to exchange personal information with each other before commencing with the negotiation. The second group came to an agreement a whopping 90% of the time. That's the power of likability.

In other words, some people can indeed charm us out of our money. This can be a spokesperson, saleswoman, or even mascot. The more likable, the more we want to *give* them our money.

Reciprocation takes advantage of the fact that when someone is nice to us, we immediately feel an emotional debt and the compulsion to pay them back. Of course, in this context, our payment back to them is a literal payment of money.

When someone does us a favor, it's natural for us to seek ways that we can perform a favor for them. This is human nature. Thus, savvy salespeople will grant you favors and take advantage of the fact that you feel an emotional pull to reciprocate the act. If someone occasionally brings you free coffee, you'll more than likely donate to their charity when the time comes. You'd feel bad if you didn't—that's emotional debt. If someone takes time out of their day for you and buys you a free lunch, you're going to feel like an ingrate if you don't let them pitch to you and sell to you afterward. You will feel a pull of debt or obligation, which is the sign that reciprocation is occurring—you don't want to do or buy something, but you feel that you *should* or *have to*.

You might give a tip of X to a good server at a restaurant. But if this very same server included a gift of after-dinner mints *just for you*, it's a good bet that you would tip more than X this time. When advertisements or salespeople appear to invest in us, it makes us feel that we should invest in them— whether we want to or not.

Scarcity fuels all things similar to "limited time offer" or "prices shoot up at midnight" or "act now because there are only three left!" This is behind every purchase that you make "just in case" or "because you didn't want to miss out." There is a ticking time bomb hanging over your head, and you are pressured into making the *safe* choice, which is to buy.

Scarcity is when you are compelled to make a decision because something seems to have low availability; it really means that you are driven by your need to not miss out on something, rather than a need to actually possess something. Scarcity makes you reactive to a situation rather than proactive. We all have useless objects we don't need because we felt that we needed to buy them before the price went up. We fear what will happen to us if we miss it; this is capitalizing on our imagination in the negative consequences (if you don't buy this product), where most advertisements tend to focus on the positive benefits and the life that could be (if only you buy this product).

Authority figures are theoretically in their positions because they know best, so we should heed their words. We listen to those in authority, no matter how arbitrary the position is, and we don't often question them. It's just how we are programmed from childhood, and this hierarchy persists throughout our lives in work, politics, sports teams, and any type of organization. There is always a chain of command, and we heed those at the top—including those who tell us to buy!

This hearkens back to the Milgram Shock Experiment from an earlier chapter, where a man in a simple white lab coat and a clipboard commanded subjects with enough authority to make them believe that they had shocked a man to death. Whenever we see someone we perceive to be in authority, we disproportionately weigh the importance of their words because we assume that they know much better than we do. We give them the extreme benefit of the doubt, regardless of whether it is deserved or earned. We listen to them because we think they know better, and if we still make a mistake, we can say that we depended on an authority figure.

Obviously, then, advertisers will either find authority figures ("leading doctors and dentists endorse this product") or paint themselves as one ("we are the world's leading authority on snails") to make you listen to their pitch for buying.

Commitment takes advantage of the fact that people like to be consistent with the things they have previously said or done. If you aren't consistent with past actions or words, then you are seen as unreliable or dishonest. For example, you would feel compelled to give a donation to charity if you were first asked if you are a kind, charitable person.

Cialdini puts it in this way: "Once people make a decision, take a stand or perform an action, they will face an interpersonal pressure to behave in a consistent manner with what they have said or done previously."

You can see that advertisers will capitalize by understanding what you think about yourself and then positioning themselves as the natural extension of that self-perception. For instance, "You did X so you're this kind of person. Those kinds of people also buy my product!"

These six persuasion methods support the fact that we are driven by subconscious emotion more than we like to admit. Purchasing is not about the prices we are paying; it's about the emotions that are evoked and eventually push us to purchase. A typical emotional decision happens extremely fast. Studies have quoted figures of around 0.1 seconds. This was necessary to activate your fight-or-flight instinct to simply keep you alive. It's what creates the "hunches" or gut feelings we sometimes have.

However, most of us (and certainly you, if you're reading this right now) don't live in that kind of world any longer. As author Jonah Lehrer put it, "The human brain (the 'rational' brain) is like a computer operating system rushed to market with only 200,000 years of field testing... [It] has lots of design flaws and bugs. The emotional brain, however, has been exquisitely refined by evolution over the last several hundred million years. Its software code has been subjected to endless tests, so it can make fast decisions based on very little information."

The logical, rational brain is relatively new and still doesn't know what to look for to make sound decisions, but the emotional brain has had millions of years of information and experience to react to. Try as we might to be impartial or coldly calculating, it's impossible to ignore the instincts that kept human beings alive. We buy out of emotion and instinct, not with a budget in mind.

The Monopoly Effect

First of all, what is *gamification* and how does it make you spend your money?

Gamification is when you apply the principles that make games addictive to non-gaming contexts. If you know what makes people feel compelled to stay up all night playing a game, you can translate those methods to make people similarly "addicted" to your product. For instance, gamification in a classroom setting would be handing out stars to children based on their accomplishments and allowing them to "level up" accordingly. This drives achievement because the kids want to keep leveling up, and the actual work itself is a part of that process.

In an office setting, you can motivate someone to work harder and make more money for the company as a byproduct of wanting to level up. For instance, let's say that for each sale someone makes, they gain a point. If they accrue enough points, their title is upgraded from sales salmon to sales tuna, then sales shark, sales whale, and sales fisher.

The idea behind gamification is to make people care about these levels and, in the process, make them care about their sales numbers. Gamification makes you want to continue something, even when you don't really want to do it. You see this all the time with points, badges of honor, loyalty programs, and prizes for those who move up in the ranks. Hint: it's not about the points or badges at all—it's about motivating people to perform the underlying action that gets them the points or badges.

What exactly does this have to do with buying psychology and sales?

It creates an extremely fertile ground for purchasing because it makes people forget about the money they are spending. Instead, it makes them focus on gaining points and gaining in general. Their reward system becomes completely rewired and turned backward because they actually feel they are being rewarded when they spend money, as opposed to feeling slight loss and regret at the expenditure of money. In order to keep advancing in levels, rewards, stages, or rankings, you must spend money—at some point, that achievement far overshadows the money spent.

Let's take a famous example that has driven literally millions of dollars in revenue: the McDonald's *Monopoly* game.

The McDonald's *Monopoly* game is a gamification strategy where customers receive stickers every time they purchase something at McDonald's. The stickers can be used in two ways. First, they could be used to complete a *Monopoly* board, and the more complete it was, the better chance you had to win a prize. Second, certain stickers by themselves bestowed rewards and gifts like free hamburgers and drinks. Right off the bat, there were two very strong motivations to spend money at McDonald's versus going somewhere else—the draw of free food and bigger rewards down the line.

For many, it became an obsession to try to complete the *Monopoly* boards or get free prizes—all of which could be accomplished by simply spending more money at McDonald's. The outcome McDonald's desired was clearly to increase its revenue, and by making people focus on progressing in the *Monopoly* game, they distracted people from the fact that they were spending much more money to get something for free than the overall value of the free item. And of course, since the game was basically like playing the lottery, McDonald's got a whole lot more revenue from those seeking to fill out their *Monopoly* boards day after day.

An important aspect was how the two rewards of free food and the *Monopoly* boards were fundamentally different kinds of gamification. The free food was a short-term and immediate reward that kept people returning on a day-to-day basis, while the completion of the *Monopoly* board was a long-term reward that kept people returning on a yearly basis—it gave purpose to the entire venture, and the food made sure that you were satisfied in the meantime. Having both rewards was critical because together they addressed short-term boredom and long-term lack of positive reinforcement.

Because of the gamification strategy employed, people ignored the fact that they were spending a *lot* on fast food for very little tangible reward—the reward was advancing in the game itself. In 2010, McDonald's increased its sales by 5.6% in the United States solely by using this strategy. It's similar to how games at a carnival can be so profitable. People will pay a sum to throw beanbags and knock down a pyramid of cans for a prize worth less than a dollar. But it's not about the value of the prize; it's about accomplishing the goal of knocking down the pyramid. That sweet feeling of advancement is a huge psychological reward. We anticipate it, then we feel it, and then we immediately seek more of it by striving to level up once more. It's addicting.

The viral mobile game *Candy Crush* was on virtually everyone's phone in its heyday. It wasn't a particularly engaging or even interesting game. The focus wasn't on gameplay or even game design. The graphics were bright and vivid, just like every other similar game. The goal was similar to the goal of *Tetris*—fill in the gaps to complete rows of three, which would open up new lanes for you to create new rows of three. At first glance, it was a completely average game, but the genius wasn't in the game itself; it was in how it made itself an addictive hit.

Candy Crush was exceedingly easy—at first. It was simple to get through the first 10 or so levels, and in doing so, people gained momentum and felt positive sentiments toward the game. No one likes a game that is too difficult or stumps you right in the beginning. That causes people to give up and is the opposite of engagement and encouragement. *Candy Crush* allowed people to get into the swing of things, feel good about their performance, and build up a reservoir of confidence about their skills. This encouraged feedback and endeared the game to people because, after all, we all like what we excel at.

As the levels began to grow more difficult and people's confidence started to waver, players started to be able to unlock bonuses, boosts, and charms that allowed them to perform better and preserve their positive feelings about the game. These boosts and charms were free, at first, but players had to pay for them later in the game. People were able to continue advancing and moving toward their goals while not feeling too discouraged about their prospects.

In order to keep the same good vibes and level of performance as before, money was becoming a requirement. As you might have guessed, the goal of the *Candy Crush* designers was to extract money from people's wallets.

The more people played, the more they would inevitably spend on seemingly useless boosts and charms because they wanted to keep playing and advancing levels. They got people used to performing well, and eventually, it became virtually impossible to advance in the game unless players started shelling out money for additional boosts and charms. A crude analogy would be what drug dealers do with their clients—they offer the first taste for free to get them hooked on the feeling, and then the dealers start to have leverage because what they have to sell is suddenly in high, high demand.

If you are enjoying a game and suddenly you feel like you have hit a wall in terms of advancement and there is an option for you to buy your way through it, you will probably take it. In fact, you will probably jump at the opportunity—and that's the essence of gamification. When you can make people spend money by distracting them from the fact that they are spending money, you'll know you did a good job.

The Legacy of Halitosis

If you are sitting on your couch and you see breaking news that a tornado is headed your way, you would probably be jolted into action and quickly run to the store to stock up on supplies. When you're in a state of fear, you want to eliminate it in any way that you can. Buying things can sometimes do that; fear in advertising captures a sliver of that jolt of fear to make you purchase, and it's nothing new.

The origins of this strategy are typically pinpointed to a 1950s Listerine ad for mouthwash. Prior to that point in time, the

153

market for mouthwash simply didn't exist. Bad breath was what it was—something that was taken care of with regular flossing and brushing, and there was no stigma surrounding it. Like many things, it was just an aspect of being a human being and wasn't thought to be particularly important one way or the other.

Moreover, at the time, the average person bathed around once a week, and deodorant hadn't been invented. Laundry certainly wasn't done on an incredibly regular basis, and people had limited wardrobes. Bodily odors were an accepted part of life. What was the purpose, anyway, if you brushed and flossed? For all intents and purposes, mouthwash wasn't something people were asking for and didn't feel that they would need.

So Listerine *invented* a reason for people to want—nay, *need*—mouthwash based on fear. Below is how their ad read:

> Jane has a pretty face. Men notice her lovely figure, but never linger long.

Because Jane has one big minus on her report card—halitosis: bad breath.

The advertisers pioneered the fear-based approach by showing Jane, who was repeatedly rejected and scared of dying a lonely spinster because of her offensive breath. The advertisements focused on how scary the effects of bad breath were and how much they could negatively affect Jane's life. Even though she was beautiful and lovely in every other regard, this one factor could ruin her romantic prospects. Listerine made bad breath a debilitating disease to which they had the sole solution, and it worked to perfection. In fact, Listerine was going to cure a global epidemic—*halitosis*. In the end, we all fear being Jane or similar to Jane, so we buy bottles of mouthwash.

Listerine invented a problem, blew it out of proportion, and then presented itself as the answer. This is a path many subsequent advertisers would take. They wanted to position themselves as the path to safety and security from fears that they shoved in your face, and when fear kicks in, human rationality is thrown out the window almost completely. When you're faced with an incoming tornado, you don't stop to think about prices of discounts—you just want to find the solution as quickly as possible. There's sudden urgency, and among the rush, money is no object. This is the perfect storm for advertisers.

A similar example of creating a fearful problem and presenting your product as the solution is how the cleaning products industry has blossomed in conjunction with widespread knowledge about bacteria, germs, and infection. Not much has actually changed in the world, but people are now generally convinced that "antibacterial" soaps, lotions, and sprays are necessary for cleanliness and sanitation.

Did the cleaning products industry create this frenzy, or did it merely capitalize on it? In television commercials, bacteria and germs were presented as miniature demons that would infect your home and spread filth and doom. These worries reached a fever pitch with random outbreaks of *E. coli*, *Salmonella*, and even SARS (avian bird flu). Today, it is common to see antibacterial soap dispensers installed in public facilities. Again, a threat was invented and the advertisers had the solution—buy my product and sleep easily at night knowing you aren't subject to bacteria and germs!

Bob Ehrlich, who helped launch the best-selling drug for cholesterol, Lipitor, stated, "Consumers remember basically one thing and one thing only," with the implication being that customers will only remember what they find scary. The unspoken fear of not a global pandemic but of miniature outbreaks of these invisible minions in your home was all that people needed to pull the trigger on buying more soap. Fear is a powerful salesperson.

Fear is one of the most primal and powerful emotions, and while this isn't without its benefits, you can see how it can be used to circumvent logic and analysis. Fear puts the priority on self-protection, eliminating threats, and acting with urgency toward perceived danger and asking questions only after the fact. Threats can come in physical, psychological, financial, or even social forms, and advertisers have to choose one to focus on, amplify, and present themselves as the solution.

Let's suppose you want to sell computers. What are the fears you might be invoking to create a small sense of panic? In other words, what are the worst versions of the negative consequences that could ever occur if you didn't own a computer?

- You could be jobless.
- You will be a social pariah.
- People will think you are stupid.
- You will miss all career and social opportunities.
- You will be seen as unsophisticated and clueless about the world.

Now, none of those are true. But it's a matter of painting a picture of despair where having a computer is the sole salvation, and suddenly people's wallets will open. What could your potential advertisement for computers sound like if you want to use fear-based advertising? Something like the following:

> Jimmy is amazing and smart, but no one knows it because he doesn't have a computer and can't communicate with anyone. He's generous and kind, but he can never get a job because he doesn't know how to use a computer. The jail cell is where he's headed. Buy Acme Computers; it's the key to avoiding poverty.

There is a final fear that advertisers like to capitalize on: the fear of missing out. Not all fear-based advertising is about the end of the world, but rather, it can be about how good your life can be and what you are not taking advantage of. Here, advertisers don't create a problem and present the solution—they create an ideal life view and present themselves as the missing puzzle piece. For instance, if someone wants to sell the same product, a computer, they would make an appeal to how a computer is the key to technology, learning, and increasing your satisfaction with life through connectivity.

In either case, fear-based advertising can make people act uncharacteristically because when people are presented with threats, logic leaves them. This is a situation that leaves people vulnerable to the psychology of buying.

<u>Be Like Mike</u>

The final piece of the puzzle in psychological sales tactics is the usage of celebrity spokespeople. It's not just the fact that we pay attention when we see a celebrity we like. We might be compelled to see a movie because our favorite star is in it, but that draw doesn't necessarily extend to products in a supermarket.

There are two main reasons celebrity endorsements are so widespread and effective, and the first one is more conventional and expected. The first reason is simply that sex sells, and celebrities often represent a paragon of masculinity or femininity. Women want to be Heidi Klum, and men want to be with her, while men want to be George Clooney, and women want to be with him. Whoever you are, you are going to be paying closer attention to an attractive figure, which means more eyeballs will be on the watch, cologne, or restaurant they are hawking. It might only be a minuscule increase in the probability of a purchase, but these things add up over time.

Sex is one of our very few primitive drives that kept us alive and thriving throughout the history of mankind. Sex and the urge to reproduce, hunger and the urge to eat, and anything else that generally kept us alive and thriving—these are all parts of what scientists like to refer to as the lizard brain, the reason being that lizards are primitive creatures that only have a few things involving survival on their minds.

The lizard brain takes over, and it turns toward impulses that suggest or show sex. Overall, this means it's tough to ignore messages and advertisements that hinge upon sex because we are hardwired to search for it and seek it out. When there's an advertisement for cologne that is being sprayed over a tanned woman's body, it might not be the most clear or informative ad—but that doesn't really matter. What matters is you are paying close attention to the sexual aspect, and the cologne itself is an unavoidable byproduct for your attention to fixate on.

You might think it's too on the nose or lacks subtlety, but studies by Dr. Jeffrey Lant have been conducted stating that we require seven distinct *touch points* (exposures) to a product before we are considered to be ready to purchase. It's indisputable that the more your eyeballs see something, the more they recognize it, mentally catalog it, and eventually want it.

Sex has been used to sell since the dawn of advertisements, but one of the first documented and widespread uses was in 1885, when W. Duke and Sons began to include trading cards of the female stars of the era on their soap's packaging. People saw the images and bought the soap to look at the pictures back at home. Did it matter to W. Duke and Sons why people bought their soap? Not at all, so long as the money exchanged hands. There's a small element of gamification here as well, because people were incentivized to collect the trading cards and spend money in pursuit of that goal.

You might be asking, what if the celebrity being used in the advertisement isn't sexy? Maybe they are best known for being funny or angry. Surely that negates the benefits of using their image as a spokesperson. That would be true if the only thing that drew us to celebrities was how handsome or beautiful they were. If that's the case, then why do we like people who are famous in spite of their less-than-supermodel looks?

This brings us to the second reason celebrities are great pitchmen: *the halo effect*.

The halo effect is a psychological phenomenon where if you see a generally attractive person (this is a subjective measure and can be physical, personality-wise, or simply someone you *like*), you will rate them more favorably in just about all traits and characteristics. For instance, if you enjoy your best friend's company, you will be more apt to rate them as attractive, honorable, funny, and creative—even if they are none of those things. The halo effect allows us to project how we feel about a person to the rest of their entire character. Obviously, this is based on an extremely limited number of data points and is overall a bit nonsensical and illogical. Just because you like someone has no bearing on if they are a smart person or not.

But as you may have noticed in this book, our brains enjoy leaping to conclusions based on the most limited of information, and it rarely looks back.

As you can imagine, the halo effect can rear its ugly head in all sorts of contexts. A teacher may treat an attractive or charming student more favorably, and a supervisor may give special treatment to an attractive subordinate. You may even pick your teammates for a sport based on how funny or good at the piano you think they are, assuming they are also physically coordinated and talented. Because the halo effect means that one good trait is supposed to lead to other good traits, the possibilities are endless.

Now, how does the halo effect make celebrities useful to advertisers? If celebrities are famous for one specific trait, we assume that this talent or ability is mentally transferred to other traits, including their taste in products. Our positive evaluations of that celebrity spread to the product itself. We trust the celebrity and their endorsement. We want to experience what they experience. We see them as experts whose leads we want to follow. And sometimes, we just want to be like them.

One of the most famous examples of celebrity endorsers is Michael Jordan, more commonly known as the greatest basketball player of all time. He was also instrumental in taking the fledgling shoe brand at the time, Nike, to worldwide prominence, as well as pitching for Wheaties, Hanes, and Gatorade, among others. People knew him as an amazing athlete, but why were we taking his advice on underwear and cereal brands? There's no logical reason he should have better taste in those arenas, yet the halo effect makes us subtly assume that the options he pitches are good—decent, at worst. *Be like Mike.*

Awareness of the halo effect may not inoculate you from its effects. Being sold to is truly a deceptive art, and advertisers are rarely trying to sell you on the features of a product. In fact, that's probably a good rule of thumb to observe—if an ad isn't about the features of the product or its literal performance and quality, then it is probably trying to tug on a psychological heartstring. The psychology of buying speaks to human desires and fears. You aren't buying a product; you are buying life improvements or avoidance of pain. That's something we'll all pay for.

Takeaways:

- A daily aspect that shows our malfunctioning brains is the way in which we react to advertisements and, in turn, the types of advertisements that are created. The psychology of buying often leads us down incorrect or suboptimal paths, and this is intentional on the part of vendors and marketers. The most important aspect they appeal to is our emotional, impulsive lizard brains. The majority of ads aren't about products and features—that in itself tells you that something else is being appealed to.
- The first way that our brains are lured into spending money is through Robert Cialdini's six methods of mass persuasion: likability (you will buy from someone who charms you), social proof (you will buy if it is endorsed by others), reciprocity (you will buy if you feel an emotional debt to repay someone else), scarcity (you will buy based on the fear of missing out), authority (you will buy based on our tendency to listen to

authority figures), and commitment (you will buy to honor a past commitment).

- Gamification is a newer tool that is being used to create addictive reactions to products. In a nutshell, it occurs when you feel that you must spend money in order to advance yourself in some sort of game or level mechanic. In a sense, gamification takes your focus off of your wallet and puts it onto the game goal that you are chasing. In this way, we spend money like drinking water.

- Fear-based advertising capitalizes on one of our most seizing emotions. Fear makes us do crazy things; advertisers seek to harness these crazy actions into spending money on their products. Fear creates urgency and a focus on alleviating or minimizing future pain— this is the most basic instinct we have as humans.

- Finally, we've all seen celebrity spokespeople. They grin at us while holding some product we would never notice otherwise. But we are looking at the advertisement now, aren't we? Celebrity spokespeople work for two main reasons. The first is plain sex appeal and grabbing our attention. The more we look, the more our buying temperature rises. Second is the halo effect, which is when we have a favorable opinion of someone and rate them highly in other traits. So when a celebrity who is not sexy is used, we buy because we rate their judgment as smart and sound.

Chapter 6. Flawed Thinking

The mistakes that our brains make are too numerous to count. You might think that this book has presented a thorough view so far—it has and it hasn't. It has shined a light on a few key areas where our brains create and operate in a world that does not resemble reality, but there are far more that haven't even been mentioned. It's almost a wonder that we can all agree on the general premises of our world given that there is so much variance in how we can experience and interpret things.

From a lack of free will to chasing superstitions and ghosts and to a memory that malfunctions more often than not, we're clearly not set up for success—if our definition of success involves accuracy and perspective. Remember, we're typically operating in the ways that our brains are accustomed to from 10,000 BC, when there were very different concerns.

Sometimes our brains are tricking us through a vestigial evolutionary tendency. Other times this is done to us intentionally, such as with the car salesman my parents encountered in the first chapter. But sometimes we just don't use critical thinking skills and fall prey to tricks and having the wool pulled over our eyes. We think stupidly most days, but most of the time it doesn't come back to bite us in the butt. Flawed thinking can sometimes be as simple as having thinking that is, well, flawed. It's either logically (consequences don't follow the premises) or perceptively (four pennies is not the same as a nickel) unsound.

To continue with the analogy, our flawed thinking can result from paying for coffee in cash and receiving your change in pennies and nickels. It seems like you have probably received the correct amount, but upon closer inspection, you might be one penny too few or too many. Still, upon first glance, you've gotten all of your money back and you can't spend the time to inspect all the pennies—so you move on with your day and you don't examine your change closely. This is similar to how our mental processes function. The misadventures of the human brain result from our divided attention and focus on creating the most complete mental picture with the least amount of information possible. As long as we're in the ballpark, we'll run with it. Imagine if you were at a pre-surgery consultation and that was the approach your surgeon had. As you might imagine, this is not the best approach to thinking. In this chapter, we'll cover a few of the most common fallacies and flaws in thinking that plague us.

First Impressions Gone Wrong

Naturally, the first place to start is with first impressions. This is where we latch onto our initial exposure or evaluation of a situation. It makes a disproportionate impact for no reason other than it being what we saw first.

For instance, if you've ever made a significant purchase in your life, such as a house or car, you'll have wondered what you could have done to reduce the price in your favor. Let's say the sticker price of the car you wanted was $20,000. You might think if you're lucky, you could get the price down to $17,000. In reality, the dealership slapped a new sticker over the old one that labeled the car as $15,000. If you are able to get the car down to $18,000, this feels like a significant win to you—and the dealership would feel the same way.

Why didn't you think you could get any lower than $17,000 and eventually settle for paying $18,000 for a car worth $15,000? Because first impressions stick with us, for better or worse.

Both parties feel good about this because the dealership presented you with a high initial price. Specifically, this was an example of the psychological phenomenon of *anchoring*.

We've all heard that first impressions are massively important when we're meeting new people. Whatever we think of someone will be emblazoned into our minds for the foreseeable future, and it may never change. With people, if we like someone right off the bat, we are willing to give them the benefit of the doubt and will allow them to get away with questionable behavior. However, if we hate someone right off the bat, we are going to attribute everything they do to malicious intent.

First impressions matter in every aspect of life. If you see a high price for a car, that is going to pervade your thoughts far more than you realize. Not only will you not feel like you can't ask for a low price, but you'll be *resistant* to the idea of a low price. You'll have it lodged into your mind that the prices simply aren't low for this type of car, regardless of whether it's true or not. You may also feel that it would be a huge social faux pas, and borderline insulting, to go drastically below the price you were quoted! You can see that you will start to convince yourself of the price's correctness.

Anchoring is a psychological effect that occurs based on first impressions. The chapter opened with an example of anchoring—the car's sticker price was $20,000, so you felt compelled to stay close to that range. Consciously, you felt $20,000 was close to the true value and couldn't deviate too far from it. Subconsciously, the initial price *anchored* you to that relative price point. Your conscious and subconscious will create a conflicted feeling which leaves you generally unable to deviate.

"Anchoring" as a term was coined in a 1974 research study (by Amos Tversky and Daniel Kahneman) that asked participants a simple question: how many African countries did they think were included in the United Nations (UN)?

This is not a question most people can answer or even have an informed estimate for, so the participants were basically guessing. Before the participants answered, they spun a wheel that had a range of numbers on it but was fixed to only land on either 10 or 65. In the context of this chapter, these numbers were indirect first impressions. You'll see that anchoring doesn't even have to be direct or blatant, as you might see in the car's pricing; it can just be something that is present in the environment that influences your evaluation.

Regardless of whether the wheel landed on 10 or 65, participants were asked the same two questions:

1. Whether they thought the percentage of African countries in the UN was higher or lower than the number they had spun.
2. What they thought was the actual percentage of African countries in the UN.

The participants who spun the wheel and landed on 10 estimated on average that 25% of African countries were in the UN, while participants who landed on 65 estimated 45% on average. It didn't even matter that the wheel was inconsequential and seemingly unrelated to the questions— the wheel provided a number that persisted in people's minds, which anchored them to either higher or lower values. Since they had no idea as to the answer to the original question, they were essentially grasping for any hint of a reference point. Without any other type of indicator or data point for guidance, they unknowingly latched onto the random number generated by the wheel and were thusly anchored.

Anchoring takes your first impression and makes you unconsciously use it as your mental reference point. It creates a set of expectations we adhere to and drastically decreases the amount of wiggle room you may have thought you had.

Let's look at another example: do you know what the population of France is? You probably have no clue. Me neither.

But suppose in one instance I told you I thought it was 20 million people and in another instance I told you I thought it was 60 million people, then asked you to estimate after each time. In the first instance, your estimate will be in the 20-million neighborhood, and in the second instance, your estimate will be in the 60-million neighborhood.

Anchoring is interesting in that it can completely skew your judgment and logic just because it's what you first see and assume is relatively accurate. We latch onto it and trust that it represents some sort of honest evaluation. You shouldn't trust your first impression, however.

When we go to a store, we see high prices that anchor us to a certain perception of value. It is much smarter for stores to keep products above a certain price sometimes so they can all anchor each other, and high prices also serve to impart a perception of quality and worth. JC Penney once attempted a dubious marketing scheme in which it introduced a "no coupons or discounts" policy in favor of generally lower pricing. They made much less revenue as a result because of their lower profit margins and the fact that people *like* discounts, and often discounts are what psychologically push people to purchase.

Restaurants have been known to engage in a practice known as *decoy pricing*, in which they place an extremely expensive item on the menu with the intention that it acts to anchor prices to a higher level and make less expensive items seem more palatable. After all, if you see a duck entrée for $50 and no other items are more expensive than $30, suddenly the other items will appear more attractive and acceptable.

The overall lesson of anchoring and first impressions at large is that people absorb information quickly and seek to make meaning of it even more quickly. It's like what people say about the Internet and other mass media—*don't believe everything that you read*. It turns out that it's hard for us to resist when it's how we're wired.

You're Wrong, I'm Right

Another way that we simply goof on thinking is through our tendency for overconfidence. Hey, a little bit of self-confidence is important, but too much can steer you straight into error after error. Recall the tragedy of the RMS Titanic, which was reputed to be indestructible to the point where there was a severe shortage of lifeboats onboard.

Overconfidence is when our brains unconsciously deceive us by telling us we are smart, we are correct, or we know better than others. Clearly, this can't be true for us all to think this way.

By necessity of statistics, 50% of us are above average, 50% are below average, and a tiny proportion of us are right in the middle, average in terms of any trait or ability. Yet why do we all prefer to insist that we aren't part of the 50% that is below average?

First of all, it's not how anyone wants to view themselves. No one thinks they are stupid; if they recognize a shortcoming in one aspect, they will find another to make up for it and still be able to consider themselves above average. It's completely natural; for instance, those who don't have academic success often say that they are instead "street smart." It might be true, but it might not. Our egos and sense of pride are desperately at work making sure we have a generally positive view of ourselves. Sometimes, however, we go too far and we protect ourselves so much that we begin to self-deceive. You'll recognize these as defense mechanisms and excuses.

Second, we know *our* thoughts and explanations for how we come to certain decisions.

If we make a poor choice or assertion, we still know we had some plausible set of reasons that made it seem not so ridiculous at the time. Essentially, we can explain and justify our faulty thoughts and decisions. When we make a mistake, it's something we accounted for and can write off as an *anomaly*. It's not something that happens often, and when it does, there was a reason for it.

However, when we look at the thoughts and behaviors of others, we can't read their minds and understand their train of thought. We only see their errors and flaws without any of the redeeming factors. We don't have any idea of why others have faulty thoughts and decisions, which means we can't justify them. It was just a bad decision made out of *stupidity*. We judge others based on bare results, while we judge ourselves based on the thought process and effort.

These two tendencies are best displayed through the *Dunning-Kruger effect*. The Dunning-Kruger effect is a psychological phenomenon where someone who is below average in a certain aspect believes themselves to be above average. In fact, the more below average they are, the more above average they often rate themselves. This occurs because *they don't know what they don't know*. They don't have the experience, context, or knowledge to recognize that they are inept or incompetent. This is a dangerous combination.

For instance, if you have just learned how to play soccer and you can complete a pass, you might think soccer is not so difficult or complex. After all, you just kick a ball, right? You possess this simplistic view because you have only been exposed to soccer as a series of kicks and passes, and you haven't seen the depth of variety in passing, strategy, and overall hand-eye coordination. Your understanding is limited to a small subset of knowledge, and thus it necessarily seems simplistic. You have no idea (though you should probably assume) that there are deeper and more complex levels. It all flies over your head, so you remain in blissful ignorance and label soccer as a simple game.

You can apply this same type of ignorance to any field—the specifics may be different, but what remains the same is that only the surface level is ever glanced at. Everything appears easy on the surface.

As another example, painting can seem extremely straightforward. You see something and you reproduce it on a paper like a printer or a photograph. That's all artists do, right? Leonardo Da Vinci and Michelangelo were just human printers. Painting and art in general appear easy until you actually attempt to do it, and only then do you start to grasp what lies beneath the surface. Your attempt at a face will look like a Pablo Picasso drawing, but not in a good way. It may be simple, but it is not *easy*, and both of those aspects matter.

The Dunning-Kruger effect originated from Cornell University in 1999, when researchers had participants perform tests of general intelligence and grammar and then rate how they thought they performed on the tests compared to the other participants. Generally, the participants who performed the worst rated themselves to be at least above average. Participants with test scores that put them into the bottom 12% rated themselves as performing in the top 62%. Conversely, people who performed above average rated themselves fairly accurately or as below average.

When you have knowledge in a certain domain, you know nothing is truly simple or easy. What someone might see as three steps is closer to 30 steps to you because you might know what's involved. If you know these steps exist, you won't be as confident in your performance or knowledge. If you don't know these steps exist, you'll be confident that you can nail three simple steps. Additionally, when people *don't know*, they don't understand the flaws in their thought patterns and fail to grasp the complexities of what they are trying to accomplish. This is why some say that those with true expertise appear to be more doubtful and less confident—because they know what they're up against.

The problem with overconfidence quickly becomes this: *how can people know when they don't know*? Well, that's a tough proposition.

This is further compounded by what's known as *confirmation bias*, which takes our inflated sense of confidence and makes it feel justified, even. Confirmation bias occurs when you start with a conclusion in mind and find the evidence to support only that conclusion.

It causes one to disregard, rationalize, deny, or steer clear of evidence that disproves or challenges that belief. It's not necessarily driven by ego so much as it is a desire for wanting to be correct—a desire so deeply rooted that your subconscious creates a filter where what you believe becomes the truth.

Confirmation bias is the ultimate stance of seeing what you want to see and using that filter to prove a pre-chosen conclusion. In fact, it's where you start with a conclusion in mind and work backward to make it your reality despite evidence directly to the contrary.

The simplest example is when you have a particular stance that you want to support—for example, that dogs are loyal. So you type into Google "dogs are very loyal"—obviously this is going to generate results about the loyalty of dogs, whereas if you type in (1) "are dogs loyal?" (2) "dogs loyalty," or (3) "dogs are not loyal," you would get a broader range of the literature on dogs and loyalty. This particular stance does not have any consequences, but confirmation bias can also turn life-threatening.

For instance, you may support the conclusion that you are a world-class skier despite the fact that you have only skied once in your life. Despite evidence that you constantly fell even on that one occasion, you explain it all away as "beginner's bad luck" and insist that you are ready for a double black diamond course—a type of course that involves steep cliffs that one could easily slip off of and slide into oblivion.

You see other people's warnings as jealous, and you even find anecdotes from famous skiers about how they were amazing after only one class, ignoring the warnings of everyone else. You find a group of first-time skiers who advanced quickly for inspiration. All your detractors "don't know who you truly are" and "underestimate your abilities." Unfortunately, you end up persisting in the belief of your abilities, and you ski right off a cliff and perish.

That's how confirmation bias can tilt your interpretation of the world by restricting the flow of information. If you want to believe an opinion, then you'll feverishly seek out sources that will buttress your belief—even if it's false. And you'll ignore ("No, I didn't see that!"), deny ("No, I refuse to believe that!"), or rationalize ("No, it's different here! *I'm* different!") sources that counteract or disprove your feelings—even if they're true.

It tends to lock us up in an echo chamber, where we only listen to a small number of the same voices and a narrow range of opinions, all of them in support of our view. For all intents and purposes, this is your world and reality; this is the majority view that seems to be the truth. With so many people (people *around* you, anyway) saying the same thing, how could you go wrong?

It's never easy (nor much fun) to be diagnosed with confirmation bias. But once you realize where it's stemming from, it should motivate you to seek a course of action to lessen its impact: *argue against yourself.*

If you're certain of your opinion, then you should be able to identify the arguments *against* your opinion. After all, you know exactly what you are ignoring, denying, or rationalizing. The typical sequence of events is that you have your opinion, an opposing argument, and then your confirmatory reaction. What then? Continue that discussion. Make an honest effort to create a back and forth to see the merits and weaknesses of both sides.

If you give 100% effort on your own opinion, you must give 100% effort on the opposing opinion. Engage with it and ask why it exists. Ask about the different perspective that created that opinion.

Question the evidence you like as harshly as you'd question the evidence you dislike. Hearing the other side of an argument will give you a much better ability to understand a different position, the different worldview or reality, and the factors involved that you never considered. Even if you don't change your opinion, you've opened up a channel that wasn't there before.

For example, maybe you're talking to someone who is bitterly opposed to the construction of a new park that you support in your neighborhood. You think a park would substantially increase the livability and comfort of your neighborhood, but your opponent doesn't think it's a good use of money.

Instead of trashing the opposing view, ask why the view exists in the first place. Maybe they feel the money's better spent on improving local roads; perhaps they'll tell a story of a relative who suffered severe injuries on a street that was in bad need of repair. Or maybe they feel that a park should only be built after other social services are fully funded and operational.

Whatever their reasoning, try to get a story from them and see if there's a solution you can work toward together.

You might find that you even start getting defensive with yourself in this process, but attempt to engage in this from a perspective of curiosity, self-education, and seeking knowledge.

An important step is to write these arguments down so you can truly see for yourself what both sides are represented by. Try outlining your viewpoints, and then make up arguments *against* them. Provide the same number of arguments for each, and directly address the corresponding ones. Flip your Google searches as we did with discovering the loyalty of dogs earlier. If evidence is presented, find it, and search for the opposite if it exists. Remember that evidence is objective, but reasoning and perspective is subjective—yours included!

After all this sweat and toil, you may find out that you don't really believe your original argument as much as you thought you did. And that's the first step to cracking confirmation bias and starting to think openly. It's the simple realization that you should leave a 1% buffer of doubt and uncertainty for yourself, and being 100% certain about something takes work that you probably haven't performed.

Our refusal to hear the opposing side isn't a sign of inner strength or resolve—it's the exact opposite. It turns out we're wrong more often than we think, and we don't have a clue—sometimes we don't even know that we don't know.

Breaking the Laws of Logic

A final element of non-flawed thinking is recognizing how the laws of logic work—or don't—in what you observe, see, and hear. Used correctly, the laws of logic will lead you straight to, well, logic. Ignored, and you will be blindfolded by flawed thinking tendencies.

By nature, the laws of logic go unnoticed. It's rare that we dissect statements from a logical perspective, and that makes for habitually sloppy arguments and poor understanding. We're just not used to it, it takes a long time, and we're lazy. So if something *sounds* credible, we deem it credible. This goes right back to how we described things at the outset of the chapter—if you are owed $0.87 and you are paid in pennies and nickels, it's good enough for you in most instances, even if it is slightly incorrect.

We've all been in conversations in which we realize that the person we're speaking with is saying something *wrong*. For whatever reason, their words don't add up. No matter, they continue and it causes a cognitive clog in your brain.

They probably think they're making sense— they don't *think* they're trying to baffle you with BS. But on the other hand, maybe they *are*. They might be trying to convolute your thinking with distorted logic and crazy talk. Whatever the case, you can't quite put your finger on what's rubbing you the wrong way and thus can't form a rebuttal. They continue to gloat and build their argument on a house of cards.

The problem isn't with your comprehension or ability to think—in fact, it's the opposite. You're dealing with someone who is *defying the laws of logic*, and while your ears are taking it all in, your brain's not having any of it. That's what causes the confusion.

But for the most part, this happens by accident in normal, everyday conversations where the people are well-intentioned. We've all done it before. We get caught up in making a firm point, get flustered if we're not convincing enough, and end up making statements that don't seem to make any sense, because they don't. We spitball on earlier statements in an attempt to salvage an argument and hope they aren't picked apart.

It's beneficial to understand the basic nature of logical thinking and construction. In the world we live in, it's a crucial mental skill to develop. It helps us ferret out the truth and process problems. It imparts the ability to parse arguments and statements and know if they need to be dealt with. This is one of Greek philosopher Aristotle's main legacies to the world.

As a quick example, a friend may be trying to remember the shoes they were wearing a particular day. They say, "If I was wearing sandals, they were red." So far, so good. They go on to say, "I'm pretty sure my shoes were red, which means I was wearing sandals." Well, that second part doesn't follow—hopefully an alarm has been set off in your brain. It just doesn't logically add up, and it's because of the structure of the statement.

Dissecting logical arguments sounds complicated, but the foundation of logical thinking is actually pretty easy to understand. The concepts are straightforward. They use sentence structure and equations to illustrate how arguments are or are not sound at their core. Understanding them breaks down to assessing the different kinds of statements people make in explaining a concept or an argument. Here, we will go over four of the most often used laws of logical statements—two of which are actually *il*logical!

Conditional statements: X -> Y. The first of our so-called laws of logic is the conditional statement. It is simply a true statement to be taken at face value. We'll use a conditional statement as the core example for all these arguments—"If you feed my dog kibbles, then he'll be friendly to you." Just to make things easy to understand, let's assume in this discussion that this statement is *always* true. There is a causal relationship.

This is called a conditional statement because it says, "*If* this condition is met, *then* this result will one hundred percent happen." The condition is your feeding your friend's dog kibbles. The result is that the dog will be friendly to you. There is a direct cause and effect relationship between the condition and the result, and it only functions in one direction—there has been no cause and effect relationship established backward.

Once again, we're pretending this will always be the case—every time you give this dog a kibble, he's going to love you.

Using this as a given, the statement is logically sound.

We also call the relationship between the condition and the result one of *premise* and *conclusion*—which are broader terms that can be used for other statements. If a certain premise is true, then you can expect the conclusion or outcome to be true.

These types of statements generally don't present as issues, unless someone is trying to pass off that the conclusion will always be true when it isn't. It's when you start to play with it that problems arise.

Converse statements: Y -> X. Now, consider this statement: "If my dog is friendly to you, it is because you fed him kibbles."

Is this true, given what we learned about conditional statements? If "If you feed my dog kibbles, then he'll be friendly to you" (*X* -> *Y*) is true, does that mean the reverse is necessarily true? Well—it's certainly a *possibility*, since we've determined that feeding the dog kibbles is a surefire way to win his friendliness. But is it the *only* way to make the dog friendly? Maybe you petted him. Perhaps you spoke to him in a gentle, friendly tone of voice. Maybe you played a game of fetch with him that made him extremely happy and he returned his happiness with intense affection to you. Maybe the dog is in a good mood. Dogs do that.

In short, no, Y -> X is often a flawed argument—an illogical statement.

This is an example of a converse statement: it reverses the conclusion and the premise or the result and the condition—it is saying that the prerequisite is true if the end result is true. And it's turned the statement into a logical flaw. It's true that feeding the dog kibbles will make him your friend. But there's no indication that he's friends with you strictly because you fed him kibbles. There are other ways you can make a dog friendly to you. You've just caught someone with their hand in the cookie jar. Remember, a statement only has cause and effect in one direction—from condition to result, and not the other way around.

A converse statement is the direct parent of something called the *false syllogism*—basically, a false premise. Its fallacy is also exposed in making leaps of judgment based on misunderstood connections like this:

- Dogs love kibbles.

- Monkeys love kibbles.

- Therefore, dogs are monkeys.

In this statement, the two premises might be true. But the fact that both dogs and monkeys like kibbles doesn't mean they're the same thing. The premise used for establishing the conclusion—mutual kibble love—is therefore false, as is the conclusion. Converse statements are where you'll catch people the most, because the cause and effect relationship isn't always examined closely.

Inverse statements: Not X -> Not Y. Okay, let's try this one on for size: "If you *don't* feed my dog kibbles, then he *won't* be friendly to you."

Really? That's the kind of dog you have? If I don't feed him kibbles—if I've run out or, you know, just don't carry kibbles on me out of habit—then he's going to turn on me? What an ingrate.

This is an inverse statement. It preserves the premise-conclusion relationship of the original statement but turns it into a *negative*: "If this doesn't happen, then this won't happen as a result." It assumes a deeper relationship between the two than actually exists.

Cause and effect certainly doesn't work if the lack of a cause means the lack of an effect.

Inverse statements are trickier because not all of them are wrong. Sometimes they're right: "If you don't brush your teeth, then they won't be healthy." Well, that's true. But it leaves out that there are other ways to make your teeth unhealthy—constantly eating food that's bad for your teeth, for example (even if you do brush).

It could very well be that the dog rejects all who do not bring him kibbles. I don't know this particular dog's neurosis when it comes to being fed kibbles at the appropriate time; I suppose it's possible it turns him into a hostile, nervous wreck.

Still, the dog may be unfriendly for other reasons. Maybe he just got back from chasing a car that he didn't catch, so he's a little disappointed. Maybe he's in a bad mood. Maybe you've insulted him. Maybe he was recently neutered. There are plenty of things that can tick this dog off besides kibble deprivation.

So while certain inverse statements might be right, not all of them will be. Be extra cautious with them and don't take them at face value. Many things will try to pass themselves off as true statements, but you can begin to see that most of them are logical flaws.

Contrapositive statements: Not Y -> Not X. These are statements that negate both the premise and the conclusion, both backward and forward. If the original conditional statement is correct, then the contrapositive is also always true, unlike the converse or inverse statements. This type of relationship does exist both ways because it's about a negative.

In our trusty dog food analogy, the conditional is "If you give the dog kibbles, then he will be friendly," and the contrapositive would be "If my dog is unfriendly to you, then you didn't give him kibbles." This is true. This is *always* true. There could be many reasons why the dog is being a jerk (see above). But one thing's for sure: if he's unfriendly, then for sure you haven't given him any of his cure-all kibbles. If you did, the dog would be more agreeable. But he isn't, so you haven't. Remember, that part is a given, so if the result is not true, then the given is also not true.

Another quick example: if you go swimming, you will be wet. What does the contrapositive statement sound like? If you are not wet, you did not go swimming. That certainly seems to make sense.

It can take a bit to decipher these types of logical statements, but once you do, you'll find that you can understand the truth of matters instantly. Our instincts make us want to skip over the details of these statements because they make sense on the surface.

There are a few other ways that X the premise and Y the conclusion are not properly accounted for in sneaky ways. These are more commonly known as *logical fallacies*, and they are errors in thinking because we simply lose track of X and Y and what matters in the first place. We'll cover two so you get a taste.

First, there is the *straw man argument*. Here's how it sounds:

Your argument (X): "This is why the gym should be closed."
Straw man (Not X): "So you're saying you're against health and for the obesity epidemic in this country?"
You (Confused as to what to defend): "Well, that wasn't really what I was saying…"

An argument is put forth, and then that argument is refuted by the straw man, which actually isn't even the same argument. The straw man suddenly and subtly changes the argument to health and obesity, where the first argument is only about the gym itself. Therefore, the straw man argument is when a false argument is created, yet treated as the same issue, to be more easily refuted. As you might guess, it's much easier to win an argument against a straw man—in this case, obesity and a nation's health.

They're hard to catch, but people love to use straw man arguments when they feel like they have nothing legitimate on their side, so they have to make their arguments about the implications, or ripple effect, and not the argument itself.

Similarly, this is how people use the same logical fallacy of the slippery slope, which often leads to a straw man argument. The slippery slope argument functions the same way. Instead of addressing the actual argument, the argument turns into the vast variety of implications that one can dream of or imagine. It is so named because a slippery slope is something people happen upon accidentally that can quickly lead to them falling down a cliff of unintended consequences.

Your argument (X): "This is why the gym should be closed."
Slippery slope (Not X): "That's a slippery slope, though. Why stop at gyms? What if you want to close hospitals and schools next?"
You (Confused at change in topic): "What do hospitals have to do with this?"

The slippery slope soon turns one simple issue into everything negative that it may remotely imply or be related to. It's a completely illogical argument to make because it sidesteps the actual topic or issue, but it's one that people use frequently. In fact, you might be the one using it to persuade people to your side, but it's a significant detriment to clear thinking if you don't realize you are doing it. You are blowing something out of proportion, which then makes it an emotional issue. Catch it and nip it in the bud, even if that means weakening your argument or stance.

Second is the *No True Scotsman* logical fallacy.

This is a logical fallacy that gives you the ability to refute just about anything by adding the phrase "But she's/he's/it's not a *real* X!" Whatever the topic is, you are redefining it on your own terms and making it so you are never in the wrong. Many people will never notice what you are doing, but they will be annoyed at how you seem to be moving the goalposts. Even if X is presented, you are changing the initial proposition to Not X.

Your argument (X): "The study said all sushi in the world has trace amounts of mercury in it."
No True Scotsman (Not a *real* X): "Yes, but no truly authentic sushi restaurant would allow that."
You (Confused by the apparent lack of acknowledgement of evidence): "Wait... did you just contradict what I just said?"

People (or you) may do this if backed into a corner. It exposes that the argument is no argument at all, and thus you adopt a patronizing tone and change the rules of the game right in front of them. In fact, you position yourself as better informed to the extent that you know the *true nature of things.*

It is a logical fallacy because it allows you to slip out of anything by embracing a new definition (Not X), despite the fact that definitions are commonly understood and generally set in stone. The No True Scotsman logical fallacy is about changing the parameters to suit you, and not address X.

These two fallacies may not be new to you, but it's important to see just how common it is to subvert the simple laws of logic we laid out earlier. Logic (or the lack of) is all around us. Sometimes we have an unconscious feel for it that makes us furrow our eyebrows, and sometimes we are fooled. Either way, it's just a byproduct of our primitive brains wanting to make decisions as fast as possible in a world that does not always reward speed.

Takeaways:

- We've established that our brains are greedy little monsters that are predisposed to thinking flaws because of their very nature. But sometimes, we just goof up on thinking and think *stupidly*. We miss connections, we misuse logic, and we simply see the world incorrectly at times. It's all part of the human experience, unfortunately.

- We are far too influenced by first impressions, mostly by the psychological phenomenon of anchoring. This creates a conflict between our subconscious and conscious and makes us unable to move from the anchor.

- We routinely think we are correct, and we are confident in our correctness. This is epitomized by two adjacent observations: confirmation bias and the Dunning-Kruger effect. We seek only what we want to hear (subconsciously), and don't know enough to know that we don't know anything (also subconsciously). You can imagine that this is a dangerous combination with regards to critical thinking and accuracy.

- Finally, it's important to understand logical arguments—especially *illogical* arguments. This is how you determine the truth and validity of what is being said. We hear these every day but may not be able to pick out their logical flaws. You can think of these as a combination of math and argumentation. There is the conditional statement (X -> Y, true), the converse statement (Y -> X, usually a flaw), the inverse statement (Not X -> Not Y, usually a flaw), and the contrapositive statement (Not Y -> Not X, true). Classic everyday examples of illogical statements are the straw man fallacy and the No True Scotsman fallacy.

Summary Guide

Chapter 2. What Free Will?

- One of the first ways our brain plays tricks on us is the illusion of free will. We want it, and most of the time, we think we have it. But we don't, because our opinions are inevitably shaped by the people around us. They can cause us to do things we wouldn't do on our own, and yet we appear to be actively choosing to engage in them. Granted, this is mostly unconscious, but can you really be said to have free will if your actions and decisions aren't completely independent? Perhaps that is a question for philosophers rather than people exploring our brain's quirks.
- The Asch Conformity Experiment showed that we are under immense amounts of pressure to fit in and avoid judgment. Peer and social pressure is a powerful shaper of not only our

decisions but what we perceive to be normal reality. It's just impossible to think in a vacuum, unfortunately.

- Stanley Milgram's Shock Experiment further showed that independent thinking is the exception rather than the rule. Specifically, it showed that the perception of authority can completely rob us of our free will, even if that authority isn't real or legitimate. We simply listen and react. All we need is a veneer of plausible deniability and innocence, and we can be pushed to extreme actions.

- The Stanford Prison Experiment demonstrated the power that instructions and roles can play in our free will. We turn out to be a product of our environments. This study, along with the others, would seem to imply that nurture wins over nature most of the time.

- Finally, we are affected by the ideomotor effect. This is a psychological phenomenon in which our unconscious desires manifest through physical action—for instance, Clever Hans the horse and the humans that would signal to him. Is our unconscious desire free will? Does free will only regard our actions? Whatever the case, it's clear that, more often than not, action does not match up to intention here.

Chapter 3. Chasing Ghosts

- We see things that don't exist, we do things that don't make a difference, and we believe in things that are fantasy. Why? Don't we know better? As always, the logical answer is yes, but as humans, we are not ruled by sense of logic and rationality. *It just feels better sometimes.* A dog probably knows he shouldn't ruin his owner's new shoes, but sometimes he just can't help it. Yes, I just compared us to dogs.
- We can't help but be a little bit superstitious. This is when we feel that an illusory cause-and-effect relationship exists. This can be caused by any number of things such as conditioning. It gives us a sense of control and certainty about the world and thus the feeling that we

can affect outcomes for ourselves. This may not be true, but it's a comforting and secure feeling versus feeling that we are at the mercy of the universe's randomness.

- We can't help but have some magical thoughts. This provides a sense of certainty in that we are able to process and understand the unexplainable— even if it is incorrect. For some of us, magical thinking arises because we are rather intuitive thinkers versus reflective thinkers—intuitive thinkers go with their gut reaction and make connections and assumptions more naturally.
- We can't help but see faces in toast, butter, and clouds. Why is that? Because of pareidolia, which is the human tendency to see patterns, especially faces, in random static noise. We see them because they help us survive and thrive—quicker pattern recognition led to quicker hunting, killing, and thinking. Now that we don't need to think in those terms most of the time, pareidolia still occurs because we are always trying to

make sense of the world by comparing it to old knowledge we possess and seeing what preexisting models it might fit.

- We can't help but see things that don't exist. Some of us have hallucinations from time to time, and they stem from three causes generally: brain problems, drugs, or visual problems. They are not features of a healthy brain, and they can occur in just about any form you can imagine. Here we are literally chasing ghosts—apparitions that don't exist.

Chapter 4. Faulty Memories

- Our brains have been proven quite imperfect thus far, and perhaps the best demonstration of this is how our memories work: poorly. Our realities are only a collection of our memories, so this is troubling. This starts from the process of creating a memory from scratch and how many steps can go wrong in that process of encoding, storing, and retrieving. But it doesn't end there.
- Next, we try to decipher the mystery of déjà vu, which is when you find yourself

in a novel or foreign situation only to feel that you've been there before. There are multiple explanations for this, ranging from a memory-encoding error to a simple forgotten exposure or a miscommunication in the brain's different memory systems. What is the real cause? We can't say yet for certain, but we can say that it doesn't allow us the gift of precognition, as some have theorized.

- False and implanted memories are another problem. You might assume that the only ways our memories can change are due to the passage of time. Unfortunately, our memories are simply not set in stone. They are incredibly malleable and flawed and can't easily distinguish what happened in reality. Thus, it is easy to create false memories and it becomes difficult to find the accurate perspective.

- Finally, the more confident we are in our memories, the less accurate they tend to be. This is shown with flashbulb memories, which are moments of time that seem to be vivid in detail and usually spurred on by an emotional impact. The problem is that when we are emotional, we are prone to thinking in ways that are anything but clear, measured, and accurate. Even though we feel like these flashbulb memories are untouchable, they decay at the same rate as normal memories.

Chapter 5. SOLD!

- A daily aspect that shows our malfunctioning brains is the way in which we react to advertisements and, in turn, the types of advertisements that are created. The psychology of buying often leads us down incorrect or suboptimal paths, and this is intentional on the part of vendors and marketers. The most important aspect they appeal to is our emotional, impulsive lizard brains. The majority of ads aren't about products and features—that in itself tells you that something else is being appealed to.
- The first way that our brains are lured into spending money is through Robert

Cialdini's six methods of mass persuasion: likability (you will buy from someone who charms you), social proof (you will buy if it is endorsed by others), reciprocity (you will buy if you feel an emotional debt to repay someone else), scarcity (you will buy based on the fear of missing out), authority (you will buy based on our tendency to listen to authority figures), and commitment (you will buy to honor a past commitment).

- Gamification is a newer tool that is being used to create addictive reactions to products. In a nutshell, it occurs when you feel that you must spend money in order to advance yourself in some sort of game or level mechanic. In a sense, gamification takes your focus off of your wallet and puts it onto the game goal that you are chasing. In this way, we spend money like drinking water.

- Fear-based advertising capitalizes on one of our most seizing emotions. Fear makes us do crazy things; advertisers seek to harness these crazy actions into spending money on their products. Fear creates urgency and a focus on alleviating or minimizing future pain—this is the most basic instinct we have as humans.

- Finally, we've all seen celebrity spokespeople. They grin at us while holding some product we would never notice otherwise. But we are looking at the advertisement now, aren't we? Celebrity spokespeople work for two main reasons. The first is plain sex appeal and grabbing our attention. The more we look, the more our buying temperature rises. Second is the halo effect, which is when we have a favorable opinion of someone and rate them highly in other traits. So when a celebrity who is not sexy is used, we buy because we rate their judgment as smart and sound.

Chapter 6. Flawed Thinking

- We've established that our brains are greedy little monsters that are predisposed to thinking flaws because of their very nature. But sometimes, we just goof up on thinking and think *stupidly*.

We miss connections, we misuse logic, and we simply see the world incorrectly at times. It's all part of the human experience, unfortunately.

- We are far too influenced by first impressions, mostly by the psychological phenomenon of anchoring. This creates a conflict between our subconscious and conscious and makes us unable to move from the anchor.

- We routinely think we are correct, and we are confident in our correctness. This is epitomized by two adjacent observations: confirmation bias and the Dunning-Kruger effect. We seek only what we want to hear (subconsciously), and don't know enough to know that we don't know anything (also subconsciously). You can imagine that this is a dangerous combination with regards to critical thinking and accuracy.

- Finally, it's important to understand logical arguments—especially *illogical* arguments. This is how you determine the truth and validity of what is being said. We hear these every day but may not be able to pick out their logical flaws. You can think of these as a combination of math and argumentation. There is the conditional statement (X -> Y, true), the converse statement (Y -> X, usually a flaw), the inverse statement (Not X -> Not Y, usually a flaw), and the contrapositive statement (Not Y -> Not X, true). Classic everyday examples of illogical statements are the straw man fallacy and the No True Scotsman fallacy.

Made in United States
Orlando, FL
29 July 2023